Deep Learning for Crack-Like Object Detection

Kaige Zhang
Postdoctoral Research Associate
Department of Computer Science
University of Minnesota – Twin Cities, St Paul, MN, USA

Heng-Da Cheng
Full Professor, Department of Computer Science
Adjunct Full Professor, Department of Electrical Engineering
Utah State University, Logan, UT, USA

CRC Press
Taylor & Francis Group
Boca Raton London New York

CRC Press is an imprint of the
Taylor & Francis Group, an **informa** business

A SCIENCE PUBLISHERS BOOK

First edition published 2023
by CRC Press
6000 Broken Sound Parkway NW, Suite 300, Boca Raton, FL 33487-2742

and by CRC Press
4 Park Square, Milton Park, Abingdon, Oxon, OX14 4RN

© 2023 Taylor & Francis Group, LLC

CRC Press is an imprint of Taylor & Francis Group, LLC

Library of Congress Cataloging-in-Publication Data (applied for)

ISBN: 978-1-032-18118-9 (hbk)
ISBN: 978-1-032-18119-6 (pbk)
ISBN: 978-1-003-25294-8 (ebk)

DOI: 10.1201/9781003252948

Typeset in Palatino
by Radiant Productions

Preface

Many books discuss computer vision and machine learning from the aspect of theory, algorithm and its applications with some simple examples that are far from practical engineering. The author worked on computer vision, pattern recognition, and image processing research over 10 years and the group leader, who is also the second author of the book, focused on making an industrial pavement surface inspection product with computer vision technology during the past 30 years. However, until 2015, there were still some tough problems in pavement crack detection that were not well solved using traditional image processing approach due to the complexity and diversity of different pavement surface conditions. Since 2015, the group focused on addressing the issue with deep learning, and soon in 2018, great progress was made and an efficient method was invented and tested on large-scale data. It is applicable to industry.

This book discusses deep learning and its applications based on a practical engineering problem: crack-like object detection. The advantage is that we conducted many tests and trials in practice and obtained many valuable engineering experiences, which cannot be found in a regular text-book. We selected five classic problems in crack detection that cover the knowledge necessary for a beginner to quickly become familiar with deep learning and how it is used in computer vision. The main research topics include image classification, transfer learning, weakly supervised learning, generative adversarial networks, fully convolutional network, domain adaptation, deep edge computing, etc. We introduce each knowledge field from the view of a practical problem and provide data and step-by-step tutorial to help the reader understand the knowledge deeply. Data and implementation tutorial could be downloaded from https:// github.com/zkghit.

Contents

1

Introduction

Cracks are common defects on surfaces of many structures, such as pavements, bridges, walls of nuclear power plants, and ceilings of tunnels (F.H.A., 2006; Amhaz et al., 2016; Abdel et al., 2003; Lad and Pawar, 2016). Timely discovering and repairing of the cracks are very important for keeping infrastructures healthy and preventing from further damage. Thus, crack detection has been a research topic in civil engineering for decades. With the increasing demand for computer-aided infrastructure inspection systems, fully automatic crack detection algorithm has attracted more and more attention in the past few decades. However, the task is non-trivial because in most contexts, the cracks appear as thin, irregular, long, narrow objects and are often buried into complex and textured background, which makes the task very challenging. In addition, in most applications, the computing platforms are on the edge with limited computing resources, which requires the algorithm to have high computational efficiency. Moreover, high accurate crack localization is an important factor to realizing automatic defect repairing in future AI systems. In this book, we discuss how to realize a computation and labor-efficient crack detection algorithm with deep learning.

During the past few years, deep learning has achieved great success and has been used to solve a variety of object detection problems. However, using deep learning for crack localization is non-trivial. First, region-based object detection cannot locate cracks accurately and it is inefficient. Second, the data imbalance problem inherent in crack-like object detection can fail the training. Third, deep learning-based methods are domain sensitive, which makes model-generalization ability poor. Fourth, deep learning is a data-driven method which relies on a large amount of manually labeled Ground Truths (GTs) for the training, that is labor-intensive and even infeasible, especially for annotating pixel-level GTs for thin cracks. Fifth, the detection system often runs on platforms on the edges with limited computing resources that require the algorithm with high efficiency.

Focusing on the aforementioned problems, the authors have spent great efforts at achieving distinct progress on the application of pavement surface inspection which is one of the most important part in pavement management system (Zhang et al., 2018; Zhang and Cheng, 2017; Zhang et al., 2020; Central Intelligence Agency, 2017; Zhang et al., 2016; Gavilan, 2011). The contents of the book are organized as follows:

In Chapter 1, we make an introduction to computer vision-based object detection, crack detection, and deep learning. In Chapter 2, we introduce deep classification network and use it to perform crack-region recognition, which realizes a rough localization of cracks from an image. In Chapter 3, we generalize the classification network to a Fully Convolutional Network (FCN) to perform pixel-level crack detection, which improves computational efficiency via preventing the redundant convolutional operations in region-based object-detection networks. In Chapter 4, we discuss a transfer learning example by fine-tuning a dilation network for crack image segmentation. In Chapter 5, we introduce generative adversarial learning and design an asymmetric U-shape network to perform end-to-end training, and the method is robust to data imbalance and biased GTs. In Chapter 6, we introduce cycle-consistent network and self-supervised learning, and show some interesting results, using crack image for image translation. In Chapter 7, we introduce some important techniques in intelligent deep edge computing that can speed up the processing on the edges.

1.1 Crack Detection in Computer Vision

Traditional low-level image processing techniques have been deeply explored for crack detection in the past thirty years. Intensity thresholding for crack image segmentation was quite popular because it was fast and straightforward. The goal was to find a proper threshold based on grayscale difference.

Chan et al. (1989) calculated the optimal threshold using edge and grayscale values based on an ideal image model with only object and background. Cheng et al. (1999) made a mapping from the intensity domain to fuzzy domain in a crack image, and designed a pavement distress detection system. Oliveira and Correia (2009) developed a dynamic thresholding method using entropy; Kirschke and Velinsky (1992) applied histogram-based thresholding to pavement image segmentation. Koutsopoulos et al. (1993) tested the Otsu thresholding method (Otsu, 1979) and the relaxation method (Rosenfield and Smith, 1979) for crack image segmentation. Alekseychuk et al. (2005) developed a dynamic optimization method for crack-like object segmentation. Zou et al. (2012) worked out an intensity difference-measuring function to find the threshold. Threshold-based methods are sensitive to noise when the background contains complex textures; however, it is very common in practical engineering applications.

More sophisticated feature extractions have also been used for crack segmentation. These methods usually work in two steps: feature extraction and pattern classification, with the first step being the key to the segmentation. Abdel-Qader et al. (2003) discussed different edge detectors for crack identification, such as Sobel, Canny and fast Haar transformation (Gonzalez et al., 2009), finding that they were too sensitive to noise. Hu and Zhao (2010) developed a crack descriptor based on a reduced Local Binary Pattern (LBP) subset that assumed that cracks could be extracted using edge, corner and plain area information, overlooking the complexity of background textures, such as the textures of pavement surfaces. Zalama et al. (2014) used visual features extracted by Gabor filters for crack detection to overcome the parameter-selection problem. They used adaBoosting to combine a set of weak classifiers (each corresponding to a distinct filter/feature-extractor) for feature extraction. Shi et al. (2016) used an integral channel feature for feature extraction and crack token mapping; named CrackForest, it applied random structured forest (Dollar and Zitnick, 2013; Kontschieder et al., 2011) to crack detection, where the distribution differences of the statistical feature histogram and statistical neighborhood histogram were used to discriminate true cracks from noise. Petrou and Kittler (1996) designed a Walsh function-based texture descriptor and built the Wigner model for crack segmentation. Wang et al.

(2000) proposed a so-called trous edge detection algorithm using wavelet transformation information of different scales for crack segmentation. Zhou et al. (2006) selected some of the statistical features based on wavelet coefficients to do the segmentation. Nejad and Zakeri (2011) developed an expert system for pavement distress detection based on the wavelet theory. However, these methods were still unable to separate crack pixels from the complicated background textures accurately because of their inability to catch the global structural information.

Because a segmented result usually contains many disjointed crack fragments due to intensity inconsistency along a crack, many methods have used some linking operations to enhance the continuity and generate elongated crack curves with less noise. Zou et al. (2012) used the minimal spanning tree to build crack curves. Vaheesan et al. (2015) used Hough transformation to enhance the connectivity of crack fragments. Zou et al. (2012) used tensor voting for such a task. Based on endpoint and orientation information, Song et al. (2015) proposed dual-threshold linking to connect the detected crack segments. By checking the connectivity along eight directions, Cheng et al. (2001) grouped and linked related crack fragments, formulating the problem as a trajectory-tracking problem, Huang and Xu (2006) connected pre-selected crack seeds along a crack path to build crack curves for crack detection. The segmentation with post-processing (noise removal and crack continuity enhancement) achieved a certain degree of success; however, it did not solve the problem well. The methods usually involved complex post-processing, in which a lot of manually tunable parameters were involved and were easy to fail when dealing with images from different sources.

1.2 Deep Learning for Object Detection

Over the last ten years, there has been great success in solving many challenging problems through deep learning (Hinton et al., 2012; LeCun et al., 2015), in which an Artificial Neural Network (ANN) with multiple hidden layers is used. Deep learning architectures can be deep belief networks, deep recurrent neural networks, Deep Convolutional Neural Networks (DCNNs), etc. For computer vision, DCNN is the mainly utilized architecture and shows great advantages for processing computer vision problems in the following three aspects. First, the convolutional kernels are learned automatically, so they have high flexibility and can mine useful information associated with the tasks by properly designing an objective function. This is impossible with traditional handcrafted feature extractors. Second, via deep architectures, the network can better catch global information by combining knowledge from different levels/scales. This is also hard to achieve using traditional handcrafted feature extraction methods. Third, the deep architecture combined with different activation functions among the hidden layers provides the ability to model complex non-linear relation between input and output which leverages the performance of processing complex pattern classification problems. With the aforementioned advantages, DCNN has dramatically improved the state-of-the-art in visual object detection.

Object detection is not only to determine what objects are in an image (object classification) but also to determine where the object is located (object localization). A milestone of the renaissance of neural network is the breakthrough of a deep classification network, AlexNet (Krizhevsky et al., 2012), which won the ImageNet Large Scale Visual Recognition Challenge 2012 (Deng et al., 2009). Subsequently, a lot of related works have been done by utilizing a deep classification network. The early works using deep learning for object detection, such as RCNN, relied on window-sliding or region proposal (Girshick et al., 2014; Girshick, 2015) to find possible image regions that contain object, and introduced a CNN to each region for feature extraction, and then sent the extracted features to a classifier, such as SVM, to determine what object it contains. Spatial Pyramid Pooling (SPP) network (He et al., 2014) calculated the CNN representation only once on the entire image and used that to find the representation for each patch generated by selective search (Uijlings et al., 2013). It needs a fixed input size due to the fully connected layers and it was realized by using a special pooling layer after the last convolution layer. Fast R-CNN (Girshick, 2015) improved SPP net by enabling gradients propagation through spatial pooling and makes the network possible to be trained end-to-end, and added a bounding box regression to the network training. Faster RCNN (Ren et al., 2015) improved Fast RCNN by replacing selective search with a small CNN, called Region Proposal Network (RPN) to generate Regions of Interest (ROI). It introduced anchor box and used different scales and aspects of ratios to generate candidate regions. R-FCN (Dai et al., 2016) introduced FCN into the Faster RCNN framework and used position-sensitive convolution for the classification. It still followed the two-stage detection ideas, region proposal and classification, but all the convolution operations were shared. Single Shot Detector (SSD) (Liu et al., 2016) did the two-stages in a single shot, simultaneously predicting the bonding box and class label when processing the image. It introduced non-maximum suppression to group highly overlapped bounding box into a single box. Similarly, YOLO (Redmon et al., 2015) divided an image into S×S grids and each grid predicts an object. An improved version of YOLO, YOLO9000 (Redmon and Farhadi, 2017), utilized 9000 object classes to train the model and introduced fully convolution and multi-scale prediction to improve the computation efficiency and detection accuracy, respectively. Mask RCNN (He et al., 2017) improved the detection accuracy by removing the Softmax layer which eliminated the competition between different classes and achieved state-of-the-art performance.

1.3 Deep Learning for Crack Detection

The early work utilized a CNN to classify an image patch as a crack or non-crack patch (Zhang and Cheng, 2017); and instead of region proposal with selective search, it used per-pixel window sliding to process a full-size image which is extremely inefficient and would cost tens of days to process a large-size image (2048 × 4096-pixel). Rather than the per-pixel window-sliding, Zhang et al. (2018) used a CNN for pre-selection which divided a full-size image into a few image blocks, and found and removed most of the background/non-crack area before performing crack segmentation within a crack patch/area. At the same time, Cha et al. (2017) proposed a CNN for block-level crack detection without post-processing which cannot localize the cracks accurately. Zhang et al. (2017) proposed a crack detection method, CrackNet, with hand-crafted convolutional kernels and also relied on window sliding to process large-size images. These methods with window-sliding are very inefficient, especially for processing large-size images because a great number of image blocks need to be processed, even introducing parallel processing (Zhang et al., 2017). To solve the computation efficiency problem, the work (Zhang et al., 2018) generalized the classification network to a detection network with fully convolutional design, and made a detailed analysis about the inefficiency of the window-sliding-based detection, and improved the computation efficiency by tens of times by eliminating the redundant convolution and performing crack detection end-to-end in one stage, in which the CNN conducted forward computation once for the process. While the computation efficiency has been greatly improved, localization accuracy is not satisfactory; and when the authors tried to further improve the crack localization accuracy by performing an end-to-end training, it failed due to the biased GTs and data imbalance inherent in crack-like object detection. At the same time, Yang et al. (2018) proposed to use a fully convolutional network for pixel-level crack detection based on images with high quality, and with carefully annotated GTs. However, as we have tested the method, it failed to process low-resolution images from industry. Similar results were also reported in the original paper of which the method failed to detect thin cracks. Targeting on building an industry system capable of processing low resolution images Zhang et al. (2021) introduced generative adversarial learning and a novel asymmetric U-shape network to handle the dada imbalance. It is also robust to biased GTs. A recent work (Zhang et al., 2020) proposed a self-supervised structure learning method for crack detection, based on cycle-consistent generative adversarial networks that do not need to manually prepare GTs for training. It minimized the human intervention, and achieved comparable results with supervised methods. It could be an important research direction of the future system for crack detection.

In this book, we introduce deep learning and object detection based on addressing practical issues for industrial pavement crack detection system because the authors have worked on the problem for decades. Nonetheless, the methods are also verified using a variety of public datasets and can be applied to other crack detection applications, and to other related computer vision applications.

2

Crack Detection with Deep Classification Network

2.1 Background

Before deep learning, crack detection was performed using image segmentation method; however, it is difficult to find a reliable threshold. The segmentation result is either with a lot of noise, or many cracks are missed; and when performing noise removal, it often removes true cracks, and when performing crack defragments, it may link the noises together to create undesirable false positives (fake cracks), as illustrated in Fig. 2.1.

Researchers have tried to solve the problem by designing various hand-crafted feature extractors and applying machine learning techniques to train a crack/non-crack classification model. In this track, Shi et al. (2016) introduced random structured forest (Dollár and Zitnick, 2013) as the classification model, and designed an integral channel feature with three colors, two magnitudes and eight orientations as feature extractors. However, the model can only collect information from a limited scope and some important global information was missed; even the statistics at different locations were combined to build an integrated feature vector, such as Hog (Dalal and Triggs, 2005). Thus, the methods cannot represent the structural information which is important to discriminate cracks from the noisy textures.

Different from traditional pattern classification method, DCNN (Deep Convolutional Neural Network) performs feature

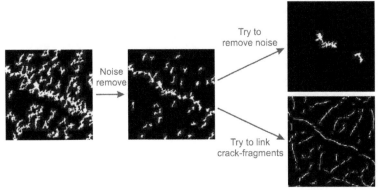

Fig. 2.1: Problem illustration with traditional crack detection methods.

extraction and machine classification end-to-end with the following advantages. First, multiple convolutional layers with different activations for feature extraction can model high non-linearity and the kernels are learned by training, which can mine more useful information. Second, deep network can include the global structural information by combining knowledge from different levels/scales, which is hard to achieve using traditional hand-crafted feature extraction methods.

2.2 Deep Convolutional Neural Network

There are two types of layers in a classic DCNN, convolutional layer and fully connected layer. For fully connected layer, each input neuron connects to every neuron in the next layer with some trainable weights. For convolutional layer, the local-connection design and weights sharing, each neuron in the next layer only connects to the neurons in a local region (see Fig. 2.2). For image processing problems, the local weights are the same as 2-D filters to perform convolutional operations on the input with some stride scale. 'Deep' means that there are multiple layers, and the convolutional layers are usually near the input, which serves as feature extractor, and the fully connected layers are at the end as a classifier. Other auxiliary designs are included between layers, such as MaxPooling (Krizhevsky et al., 2012); ReLu (Nair et al., 2010), Dropout (Srivastava et al., 2014; Wan et al., 2013), etc. With such a setting, DCNN can extract representative features for image classification, object detection, image segmentation, etc.

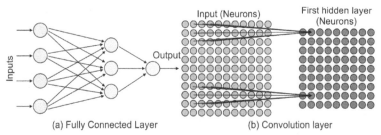

Fig. 2.2: Fully connected layer and convolutional layer.

2.3 Transfer Learning

In deep learning, the challenge is to train the network. A deep neural network usually has tens of millions of parameters. For example, AlexNet (Krizhevsky et al., 2012) has 60 million and VGG (Simonyan and Zisserman, 2014) has 138 million. Training such networks requires a large amount of labeled data; however, it is not easy to prepare the data with sufficient size. Fortunately, people find that through transferring the knowledge learned from a different task and fine-tuning the network with limited data, the network can converge, and such strategy is named transfer learning. Following the definition by Pan and Yang (2010), given a source domain D_s and a learning task T_s, a target domain D_t and a learning task T_t, transfer learning intends to improve the learning of the target predictive function $f_t(\cdot)$ in D_t by applying the knowledge in D_s and T_s, where $D_s \neq D_t$, or $T_s \neq T_t$. Depending on the situations between the source and target domains and tasks, inductive transfer learning and transductive transfer learning are defined as follows (Pan and Yang, 2010):

In inductive transfer learning, the target and source tasks are different, regardless of the similarity between the source and target domains, which means that the aim is to improve the learning of $f_t(\cdot)$ in D_t applying the knowledge in D_s and T_s, where $T_s \neq T_t$. In transductive transfer learning, the source and target tasks are identical, but the source and target domains are different. In other words, transductive transfer learning intends to improve the learning of $f_t(\cdot)$ in D_t applying the knowledge in D_s and T_s, where $D_s \neq D_t$ and $T_s \neq T_t$. Yosinski et al. (2014) discussed the transferability of knowledge from different layers in deep convolutional neural network. In general, low-level convolutional layers learn more generic features with strong transferability and higher-level layers learn knowledge more specific to the task. In this chapter, we discuss transferring the generic knowledge from a pre-trained network using ImageNet data (Deng et al., 2019) and fine-tuning the network to discriminate crack and non-crack blocks for pre-selection.

2.4 Crack Detection with Deep Classification Network

2.4.1 Pre-selection with Transfer Learning

Traditional image segmentation cannot handle the noise problem well. It is straightforward to introduce deep learning to screen out the noisy background before crack segmentation. A deep convolutional neural network with five convolutional layers and two fully connected layers is used. The convolutional layers are trained to find proper kernels for feature extraction, and the multi-layer deep architecture is used to get the global structural pattern. The generic knowledge from a pre-trained model is transferred for the training.

In the experiment, 600 pavement images (2048×4096-pixel each) with low similarity are selected from 20,000 images. Among them, 400 images are used to obtain the training set of 30,000 crack blocks and 30,000 background blocks of 400×400-pixel. The images are further used to generate sub-blocks of 200×200-pixel by cropping from the center. The other 200 images are used to produce test set of 20,000 crack and 20,000 background image blocks. As shown in Fig. 2.3, the image blocks are generated as follows:

- For each image of 2048×4096-pixel, cracks are manually marked by 1-pixel-width curves.
- Crack blocks are sampled from the original images along the crack curves, and the background blocks are sampled randomly from the background.
- To reduce similarity, the distance d between two block samples satisfies $d > w/2$, where w = side length of the sample block.

Image resizing and image rotation are used to augment the data and increase the variability because (1) cracks are direction invariant; and (2) different cracks may have different widths, and

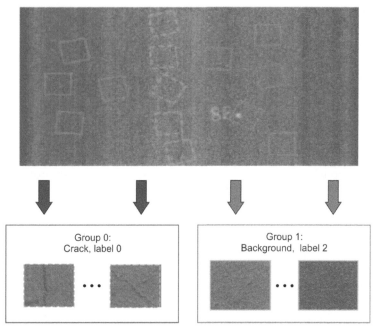

Fig. 2.3: Illustration of image-block generation.

the background textures might have different coarse levels. Thus, image rotation and image resizing are used for data augmentation.

A DCNN usually contains tens of millions of parameters. Directly learning such a huge number of parameters is very challenging. It has been verified that the knowledge learned from one task can be used to ease the network training of other tasks (Pan and Yang 2010; Oquab et al., 2014); that is, the learning of a task can be improved by using the knowledge learned from other tasks, and the improvement is significant in large-data driven tasks, such as deep learning. Typically, the generic features, such as edge and color blobs, occur at a high probability regardless of the exact cost function and data (Yosinski et al., 2014). In DCNNs, low-level convolutional layers learn more generic features and higher-level layers learn knowledge more specific to the task (Pan and Yang, 2010). Before transfer leaning, three problems are important: what knowledge to transfer, how to transfer, and when to transfer. Here, only the generic knowledge in the first convolutional layer is transferred from the pre-trained model

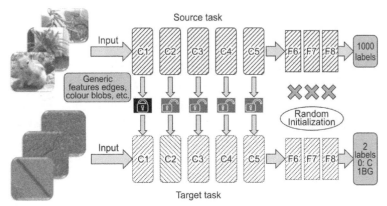

Fig. 2.4: Transfer of generic knowledge based on ImageNet data (C1, C2, C3, C4, and C5 = five convolution layers; F6, F7, and F8 = three fully connected layers; C = crack, BG = background).

(Deng et al., 2009). As shown in Fig. 2.4, the lock between two C1 layers indicates the transfer of generic features from convolution kernels, which are fixed during training. The locks between C2, C3, C4, and C5 indicate fine-tuning, and the × between F6, F7, and F8 indicate that no knowledge is transferred. The settings are based on the following considerations:

- The crack patterns are relatively simple which can be represented by the generic knowledge,
- The crack patterns have little similarity with the natural objects (e.g. dog, cat); therefore, middle-level and high-level knowledge is less useful for crack detection; and
- Transferring the generic features from low-level layer making the network training easier.

In Fig. 2.4, the source network is pre-trained with Caffe (Jia et al., 2014). The model takes an image block as input and produces a probability distribution over 1,000 object classes. The network has five convolutional layers (C1, C2, C3, C4 and C5) followed by three fully connected layers (F6, F7 and F8). The convolutional layers serve as feature extractor. The fully connected layers serve as a classifier to produce class labels by computing $Y_6 = \sigma(W_6 Y_5 + B_6)$, $Y_7 = \sigma(W_7 Y_6 + B_7)$, and $Y_8 = \varphi(W_8 Y_7 + B_8)$, where Y_k denotes the output of the k-th layer, W_k and B_k are trainable parameters of the k-th layer; and $\sigma(X[i]) = \max(0, X[i])$ and $\varphi(X) = e^{X[i]} / \sum_j e^{X[j]}$ are

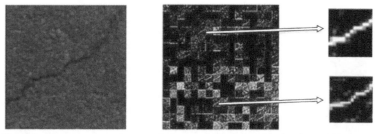

Fig. 2.5: Feature maps of a sample image. Left: Image block of 227×227 pixels. Right: Feature maps after the process of first convolutional layer.

ReLU and SoftMax activation functions, respectively. Stochastic Gradient Descent (SGD) (Rumelhart et al., 1986) is used to update the parameters during training. In the target task, pavement image blocks are input into the network, and are resized to 227×227-pixel for training. The first lock on the left shows that the generic features learned from the first convolutional layer C1 are transferred directly and kept unchanged during training; the other four locks indicate that the parameters from C2, C3, C4 and C5 are copied from the source network but are allowed to change during training, which means that the higher-level knowledge is relearned for the target task. The parameters of the last three fully connected layers, F6, F7 and F8, are randomly initialized and trained by SGD (Rumelhart et al., 1986). Figure 2.5 shows that the network is able to extract useful crack information.

Based on transfer learning, a pavement image is first divided into smaller image blocks. As shown in Fig. 2.6, if a crack travels through the center area of a block, the block is classified as crack; if the crack is near the border of the image block, it is classified as background. Specifically, an image block with a crack traveling outside the center area with $w_c = 100$ is classified as background. In addition, the size of the image block can influence the classification performance: the smaller it is, the less object global information it has, which makes the classification more difficult. The larger the image block is, the more background regions are involved, which makes the pre-classification less useful. In addition, if the image was large, crack information could be lost when we resize the image to 227×227-pixel. Based on such considerations, a two-step pre-selection is used in our early work. First, a mask block is defined, and it is a smaller image region with side length

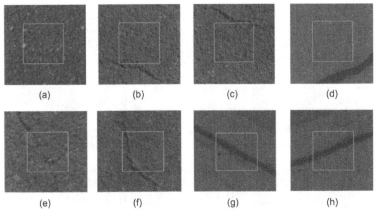

(a)   (b)   (c)   (d)

(e)   (f)   (g)   (h)

Fig. 2.6: Classification results for different image blocks; squares indicate mask blocks: (a – d) background; (e – h) crack.

$w_c = w/2$ (Fig. 2.6), and it is used to locate the crack region in the mask image. The mask image is defined as a binary image with the same size as the original image which uses 1s to represent crack and 0s to represent background. Considering efficiency and accuracy, the two-step pre-selection is executed. In the first step, 400×400-pixel image blocks are sampled from the original image sequentially, and they are input into the DCNN. The step-size d_s is 100 pixels with overlapping between adjacent samples. If the image block is classified as crack, the related mask block area in the mask image is set to 1. In the second step, sampling of 200×200-pixel blocks with a step-size of 50 pixel is conducted, focusing only on the crack regions to obtain more accurate areas with mask sizes of 100×100-pixel. In such a way, the mask images are generated and most of the noisy background regions are detected and discarded. The cracks are separated and located in 100×100-pixle mask block area to assist crack segmentation and extraction. Figure 2.7 shows the results for some example images.

2.4.2 Crack Curve Extraction

After pre-classification, cracks can be located in 100×100-pixel areas. To obtain more accurate crack locations to facilitate statistics (Wang, 2015; Hawks and Teng, 2014), a crack curve extraction method can be applied. First, a block-wise

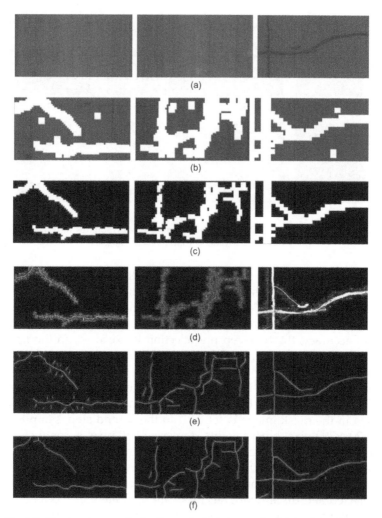

Fig. 2.7: Step-by-step results for the crack detection method: (a) original images; (b) results after first step of pre-selection; (c) mask images after second step of pre-selection; (d) results for block-wise segmentation; (e) results for curve detection; (f) final results for detected crack curves.

segmentation is performed, based on linear regression which is optimized with Least Absolute Shrinkage and Selection Operator (LASSO), and then tensor voting is used to extract the final crack curves.

Linear regression is a widely used method in machine learning. Suppose there are n observations $\{x_i, y_i\}_{i=1}^{n}$. Each observation includes a response variable y_i and a column vector x_i of p predictors. The mathematical expression of the ordinary linear regression model is:

$$y_i = \beta_1 x_{i1} + \beta_2 x_{i2} + \cdots + \beta_p x_{ip} + \varepsilon_i \qquad (2.1)$$

The target is to find the 'best' coefficients β that minimize the objective function S:

$$S(\beta) = \sum_{i=1}^{n} |y_i - \sum_{j=1}^{p} x_{ij} \beta_j|^2 \qquad (2.2)$$

A popular method called 'ridge regression' is to improve the ordinal linear regression by making a L2 norm constraint to the objective:

$$S(\beta) = \sum_{i=1}^{n} |y_i - \sum_{j=1}^{p} x_{ij} \beta_j|^2 + \lambda \, \|\beta\|^2 \qquad (2.3)$$

Least Absolute Shrinkage and Selection Operator (LASSO) (Tibshirani, 1996) replaces the constraint with L1 norm and the objective:

$$S(\beta) = \sum_{i=1}^{n} |y_i - \sum_{j=1}^{p} x_{ij} \beta_j|^2 + \lambda \, |\beta| \qquad (2.4)$$

As shown in Fig. 2.8, LASSO tends to force the coefficients of the least influential features to be exactly zero. The blue diamond denotes the LASSO constraint with L1 penalty and the blue circle is the ridge regression with L2 penalty, respectively. The optimization is equal to expanding the red ellipse gradually until touching the L1 or L2 constraint area. From Fig. 2.8, the coefficient estimations of LASSO and ridge regression are given by the point at which the ellipse first touches the diamond/circle region. For LASSO, the first contacted point will be the one located at some axes where some of the coefficients are zero; while for ridge regression, the point will be somewhere at the boundary of the circle. Thus, LASSO could be used for variable/feature selection. The segmentation is realized by using a thresholding method where a linear regression model is used to find the proper threshold for each block. In detail, 2,000 low similarity image blocks, each of 100×100-pixel, are collected; the related statistics and the best threshold for each block are then calculated and used to fit a linear model as discussed subsequently. The best threshold

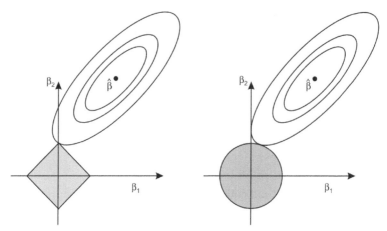

Fig. 2.8: Illustration of the difference between ridge regression and LASSO.

is defined as the one that maximizes the F_1 measure (Power, 2011) of the segmented result against the ground truth of each image block; it can be obtained automatically by comparing the segmented results, using different threshold values with the GTs (the values from M-30 to M+30 are used, M is the mean value of the block); the threshold value maximizing the F_1 measure is selected as the best threshold for that block. The related statistics are mean (M), standard deviation (SD), smoothness (SM), third momentum (TM), and uniformity (UF). The linear model is

$$T = \beta_0 + \beta_1\,M + \beta_2\,SD + \beta_3\,SM + \beta_4\,TM + \beta_5\,UF \quad (2.7)$$

where $\beta_0, \beta_1, \ldots, \beta_5$ = parameters to be determined by least square formula. It is well known that the stability and prediction accuracy of a linear model are heavily related to the selected predictors (Sheather, 2009); here, the LASSO are used. The constraint of the least squares is

$$\min\Sigma_{i=1}^{n}(T_i - \{\beta_0 + \beta_1\,M + \beta_2\,SD + \beta_3\,SM + \beta_4\,TM + \beta_5\,UF\})_2 \quad (2.8)$$

subject to

$$\Sigma_{j=1}^{5}\mid \beta_2 \mid\, < s \quad (2.9)$$

where s is constant; and $s \geq 0$. By using the Lagrange multiplier, it is equivalent to minimizing the residual sum of the squares plus a penalty term as

$$\min\Sigma_{i=1}^{n}(T_i - \{\beta_0 + \beta_1 M + \beta_2 SD + \beta_3 SM + \beta_4 TM + \beta_5 UF\})_2 + \lambda \quad (2.10)$$

where $\lambda \geq 0$. When s is small (or equivalently λ is large), some of the regression coefficients will approach 0, which serves to eliminate the predictors that are not significant. As shown in Fig. 2.9, λ is set as 0.729 by the minimum-plus-one standard error formula, achieving a good R^2 (0.68) (Friedman et al., 2010). Finally, M, SD and UF are selected as the most significant predictors, and the prediction model is

$$T = 1.11 * M - 1.21 * SD + 0.33 * UF - 5.52 \quad (2.11)$$

In addition, the performance of other thresholding methods, including Otsu and Zou et al. is compared; both achieved lower R^2 (0.30 for Otsu (1975) and 0.41 for Zou et al. (2012)). The related segmentation results are shown in Fig. 2.10. Focusing on the

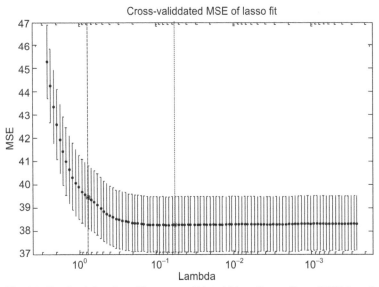

Fig. 2.9: Best lambda selected by cross-validated Mean Square Error (MSE) based on minimum-plus-one standard error formula (solid line to left = lowest value achieved by MSE; solid line to right represents minimum-plus-one standard error, which is also the lambda chosen by LASSO).

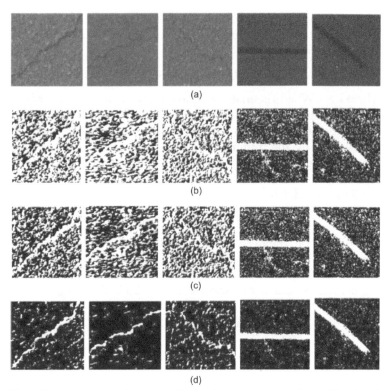

Fig. 2.10: Comparison of segmentation methods on image blocks: (a) original crack image blocks; (b) segmentation results using (Otsu, 1979); (c) segmentation results using (Zou et al., 2012); and (d) segmentation results for proposed method.

crack block-regions, the best thresholds are calculated using Eq. (2.11), and the thresholding is conducted to obtain the segmented blocks and to produce the segmented binary images as in Fig. 2.7(d). Then a crack curve extraction is conducted. As shown in Fig. 2.7(d), the segmented results may contain many discontinuous crack fragments and noises; therefore, tensor voting-based curve detection (Medioni and Tang, 2000) is used to connect the crack fragments along some curves and produce crack curves with less noise. Notice that there are some small gaps in the curves generated by using the local maximum voting strength (Linton, 2017). Therefore, a gap-filling operation using the morphology close operation (Gonzalez et al., 2009) is applied to connect crack segments if the nearest distance among them is less than 10 pixels.

2.4.3 Experimental Results

The experiments are performed by using an HP Z220 workstation with 16G memory; an Nvidia 1080TI GPU is used for training and testing. The dataset is obtained from the images captured by a line-scan camera mounted at a height of 2.3 m on the top of a vehicle; the camera can scan a 2 × 4-m road area to generate a 2,000×4,000-pixel image (i.e., a road area of 1 mm² corresponds to 1 pixel). The vehicle can work at 100 km/h. Detection performance is compared with that of four methods in terms of recall, precision and F_1-measure. Precision and recall can be computed by using true positive (TP), false negative (FN) and false positive (FP):

$$Precision = \frac{TP}{TP + FP}, Recall = \frac{TP}{TP + FN}.$$

The source network is pre-trained with ImageNet data. The input image block is resized to 227×227 pixels, and the generic knowledge is transferred by copying the parameters. The base learning rate *base_lr* is 0.001, the test iteration is 100, and min-batch is 400. The learning policy is that for every step-size (100 is used) iterations, the learning rate decreases to lr_{step} = *base_lr* * *gamma*^floor(iter/step). Here, lr_{step} = learning rate after *iter* iterations, *iter* = current iteration time, *step* = step size, *base_lr* = base learning rate, and *gamma* = decreasing factor. Weight decay is set as 0.005 and all weights of the convolutional layers are copied from the pre-trained source network. The output labels of the last layer are 0 and 1 representing C (crack) and BG (background), respectively. The maximum iteration time is 40,000.

For evaluation of the detection, the proposed method is compared with traditional edge detection methods, Canny, CrackIT and CrackForest. In the experiments, the GTs of 300 test images are manually marked. As shown in Fig. 2.11(c), Canny segmentation cannot obtain any intuitive cracking information because it is too sensitive to noise and it achieves high recall (0.999) but very low precision (0.001). CrackIT cannot detect cracks because of the low resolution and low contrast of the industrial pavement image, Fig. 2.11(d); consequently, both recall and precision are very low (0.001). CrackForest shows good detection property via its crack mapping strategy by using random forest; however, it cannot cope with noise, especially the noise connected

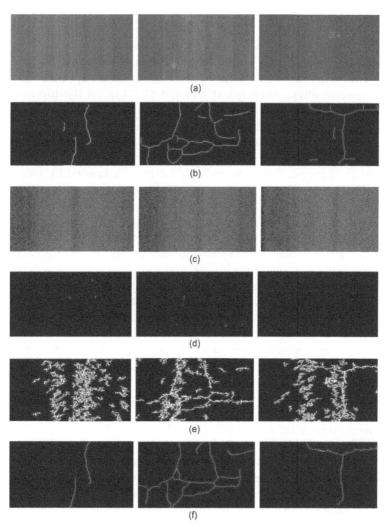

Fig. 2.11: Comparison of results using actual industry images: (a) original pavement images; (b) manually marked GTs; (c) Canny; (d) CrackIT; (e) CrackForest; (f) proposed method.

to the true crack regions; also, it achieves low precision (0.515). Table 2.1 summarizes the statistical results.

Table 2.1: Performance evaluation.

Method	Recall	Precision	F_1-measure
Canny	0.999	0.001	0.002
CrackIT	0.891	0.252	0.490
CrackForest	0.851	0.515	0.641
Proposed method	0.951	0.847	0.895

2.5 Summary

In this chapter, a deep classification network is introduced to perform pre-selection which removes most background areas before crack segmentation, based on a window-sliding strategy. We have presented that the generic knowledge learned from ImageNet contains rich structural information and it can be used to extract crack patterns for crack/non-crack classification. The pre-classification using deep convolutional network outperformed the hand-crafted feature extraction method, which also indicated that the global information is important to discriminate cracks and complicated background textures. The approach is our work in 2016, and the computational efficiency remained an issue at that time.

3

Crack Detection with Fully Convolutional Network

3.1 Background

In Chapter 2, we introduced a deep classification network to perform a pre-selection that removed most noisy background regions to assist crack detection and achieved very good results. It is a region-based object-detection method where window-sliding is needed when processing large input images. However, the window-sliding-based processing is very inefficient when dealing with a large-size image. Such a problem is a serious issue of deep learning-based object detection, but is rarely mentioned in the early times; for example, the time cost of processing an industrial pavement image, 2048×4096-pixel, is 20 seconds with window sliding. In addition, the method employed complex post-processing to extract a crack curve for the detection which is time consuming as well. In this chapter, we discuss the reason behind the method and propose a one-stage crack detection approach based on Fully Convolutional Network (FCN).

3.2 Fully Convolutional Network

Before FCN, DCNN (Deep Convolutional Neural Network) based methods were restrained by the condition that the input image has to be of a fixed size and once the training is finished, it can only deal with images with the specific size, or the inputs have to be resized (Girshick et al., 2014). The reason is that the fully connected layer requires a fixed input dimension. However, it turns out that the fully connected layer can be treated as a special case of the convolutional layer with kernel size equal to the entire input dimension. Long et al. (2015) proposed fully convolutional network for per-pixel semantic segmentation. It implements an end-to-end, pixel-by-pixel, supervised learning by introducing some up-sampling strategy to handle the resolution loss. Instead of paying attention to building an end-to-end network with up-sampling, we introduce the fully convolutional design to convert a classification network into an object-detection network to process full-size images seamlessly (Zhang et al., 2018). More importantly, our work shows that semantic segmentation can be realized by a classification network working under a larger field of view, and this can explain many phenomena with fully convolutional network, such as the boundary vagueness in semantic segmentation (Long et al., 2015), blurring of generated images using GAN (Generative Adversarial Network) (Isola et al., 2017).

3.3 Dilated Convolution

The dilated convolution was originally designed for end-to-end semantic segmentation by aggregating contextual information at multi-scales (Yu and Koltun, 2016; Chen et al., 2015; Chen et al., 2017). Figure 3.1 considers 2-D discrete convolution as: let $F: \mathbb{Z}^2 \to \mathbb{R}$ be a 2-D discrete function with domain $\Omega_f = [-f, f]$, which can be viewed as the input image, and let $K: \mathbb{Z}^2 \to \mathbb{R}$ be another 2-D function with domain $\Omega_k = [-k, k]$, which can be viewed as the convolutional kernel, assuming $n < m$. The discrete convolution operator $*$ can be expressed as:

$$F * K(m,n) = \sum_{i=-r}^{r}\sum_{j=-r}^{r} F(m-i, n-j)K(i,j) \tag{3.1}$$

For the dilated convolution, the kernel function is changed to

$$K_{i,j}^{d} = \begin{cases} K_{i/s,j/s}, & \text{if } s \text{ divides } i \text{ and } j; \\ 0, & \text{otherwise.} \end{cases} \tag{3.2}$$

From Fig. 3.1, with dilated convolution, the receptive field is expanded directly which can involve much more contextual information; and it is reported that via such a way, the network can achieve better performance for semantic segmentation problems (Yu and Koltun, 2016). However, instead of emphasizing the

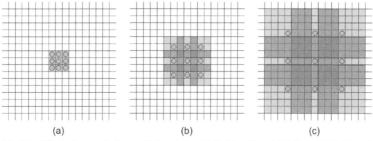

(a)   (b)   (c)

Fig. 3.1: Dilated convolution with kernels of 3×3: (a) without dilation; (b) 2-dilated convolution; (c) 3-dilated convolution (Yu and Koltun, 2016).

significance of enlarging the context coverage in an end-to-end training mode, our work presents that dilated convolution is an equivalent implementation of the standard convolutions with dense inter-sampling under multi-layer CNN context that can be used to enable the transfer of middle-level knowledge and facilitate the end-to-end training.

3.4 End-to-End Crack Detection with FCN

In our early experiments, it was found that training an FCN (Long et al., 2015) for end-to-end per-pixel crack detection was difficult. The possible reasons are: (1) crack can only occupy a very small area in the full image compared to the background; with the fact that patch-wise training is equivalent to loss sampling in FCN (Long et al., 2015) which is directly applied to pavement crack image for pixel-level detection and is same as operating on an unbalanced training dataset. (2) The precise GTs of pavement crack images are inherently difficult to mark. That makes the per-pixel GT inaccurate. Therefore, the community usually makes GTs by marking the cracks with 1-pixel curves. While such GT is more than welcome by the engineers, however, they cannot perfectly match the actual crack at pixel-level, making the computation inaccurate.

We first train a classification network with transfer learning for the classification of crack and background image blocks. The initial classification network with fully connected layers can only process image blocks with a fixed size. Then, for an end-to-end crack detection network, we replace fully connected layers with fully convolutional layers. While the convolutional layer does not

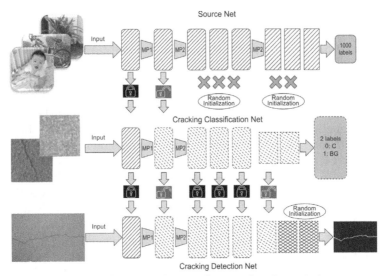

Fig. 3.2: Overview of the proposed approach: network at the top is the source net trained with ImageNet; network in the middle is the crack block classification net trained with transfer learning and network at bottom is the proposed dilation net for crack detection (C=crack; BG=background).

require a fixed input, the network can work on full-size image directly to produce a low resolution output with rough crack localization information. Since the resolution decrease mainly comes from the operations working at the stride larger than one, we set the stride as one and introduce dilation to remedy the affection of stride changes. Figure 3.2 presents an overview of such a design.

Compared with the task for high accurate crack localization, training the network for image-block classifier is much easier. The classification can be viewed as a weak supervised detection, and is important for transforming the classification network into detection network. The data used to train the classification network are prepared by following the data augmentation strategy in Chapter 2 and transfer learning is used. In essence, the DCNN involves many filters that conduct convolution operations on various input images for feature extraction. However, each of the convolution kernels actually operates on the entire image (or the entire feature maps) which makes the convolutional layer have more chances to extract the common features or knowledge. Specifically, for the lower convolutional layers, they usually learn generic knowledge that has strong transferability. As in Chapter 2, a pre-trained model is used as the source network, and the generic knowledge from low-level convolutional layers is transferred by initializing the parameters with the pre-trained model. In the experiments, it re-implements the network by (1) transferring the generic knowledge by copying the weights of the first convolutional layer; (2) removing the max-pooling layer between C5 and F1; (3) removing F3 and halving the output channels of C3, C4, C5, C6, F1 and F2 for parameter reduction. The weights of C2 are copied from the source net and retrained; weights of C3-C5, F1 and F2 are randomly initialized and trained. The inputs are image blocks with the labels of crack and background. In the last layer, Softmax layer (Krizhevsky et al., 2012) is employed to calculate the loss, and the gradient information is sent back to the former layers for parameter updating via back propagation (Rumelhart et al., 1986). In this way, it can create a well-trained classification network.

An ideal method using a classification network to perform detection is the patch-wise per-pixel labeling, but the time cost is unacceptable because it conducts the forward computation at every pixel, patch-by-patch. Researchers have tried to find a trade-off by using region proposal and stride window-sliding (Girshick et al., 2014; Girshick, 2015; Redmon et al., 2015; Sermanet et al., 2014); however, it is still not good for large image processing. In this chapter, we propose a solution by introducing equivalent convolutional layers to replace the fully connected layers and designing an equivalent dense dilation layer to transform a classification network to an end-to-end detection network.

As shown in Fig. 3.3, a fully connected layer can be replaced by an equivalent convolutional layer. Assume that there was a layer with $m \times m \times 1$-dimension feature map as input, and the number of neurons in the next layer is M. For the fully connected layer, the $m \times m$ feature map will be treated as an $m^2 \times 1$ vector with each element as an input neuron, and they are connected to every neuron in the next layer independently. For equivalent convolutional layer, we can configure M convolutional kernels, each with $m \times m \times 1$-dimension, and which conduct convolution on the entire input respectively. The output would be M-dimension

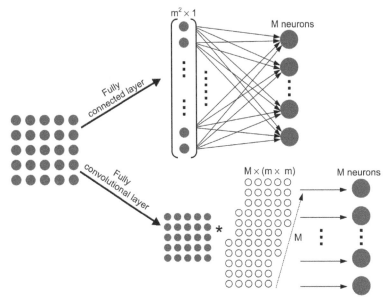

Fig. 3.3: Fully connected layer is a special case of the convolutional layer.

feature map, and each of the map is in 1×1-dimension. It is a different implementation, but the function is the same. Here, the dimension property of a layer is defined as a vector with three elements representing input, trainable parameter and output dimension. D_{fconn}, $D_{\text{fconn}} = (m^2 \times 1, m^2 \times M, M)$, and D_{fconv}, $D_{\text{fconv}} = (m \times m, M \times m^2, M)$, denote the dimension of a fully connected layer and the dimension of a fully convolutional layer, respectively. The dimension equality of the two implementations is as illustrated in Fig. 3.3.

In the classification network, the input dimension of the first fully connected layer F1 6×6×128 from C5 ($m = 6$), and the output is 2048 neurons (M = 2048). Thus, we can apply 2048 convolution kernels of 6×6×128-dimension on the feature maps and produce 2048×1-dimension output to match the original F1 layer. For F2, since the input has a 1×2048 dimension 'feature-map', we can use a 1×1×2048-dimension kernel and set the output as a 3-dimension. Table 3.1 shows the dimension details. Since the convolutional operation does not require a fixed input size, the modified network can work on the full image directly without retraining the parameters.

Table 3.1: Network setting and output dimensions.

Network	Property	1	2	3	4	5	6	7	8	9
Classification Net		The same with the Naive Detection Net below except that the input size is 227×227 and output 3-dimension category labels.								
Naive Detection Network	Operation	Conv. & MP	Conv. & MP	Conv.	Conv.	Conv.	Conv.	F-Conv.	F-Conv.	--
	Spatial Input	2000×4000	250×500	125×250	125×250	125×250	125×250	63×125	63×125	--
	Filter Dim. & Stride	11×11×96 & 4	5×5×256 & 1	3×3×192 & 1	3×3×192 & 1	3×3×128 & 1	3×3×128 & 1	6×6×2048 & 1	1×1×3 & 1	--
	Pool Size & Stride	3 & 2	3 & 2	--	--	--	--	--	--	--
Dense Dilation Network	Operation	Conv.&MP	Conv.&MP	Conv.	Conv.	Conv.	Conv.	F-Conv.	F-Conv.	F-Conv.
	Spatial Input	2000×4000	250×500	250×500	250×500	250×500	250×500	250×500	250×500	250×500
	Filter Dim. & Stride	11×11×96 & 4	5×5×256 & 1	3×3×192 & 1	3×3×192 & 1	3×3×128 & 1	3×3×128 & 1	6×6×2048 & 1	3×3×1000 & 1	1×1×3 & 1
	Pool Size & Stride	3 & 2	3 & 1	--	--	--	--	--	--	--
	Dilation	--	--	2	2	2	2	4	--	--

Before implementing a detection network for large size images, we make an analysis of the resolution changes under a large input. Assume that a classification net is trained, based on images with size $m \times m$-pixel. We directly apply the convolutional network on images with sizes M×M-pixel, where M>m. At first glance, it tends to give us an illusion that the network realized a 227-time down-sampling process since the input is a 227×227-pixel image and the output is a classification label. If so, the classification net working on full-size image tended to produce an output with resolution = (2000×4000)/227 = 8.8 × 17.6. However, it is not true! As in Table 3.1, it got a 63×125 output. Indeed, under a larger field of view, such FCN-based design actually realized multiple-spot detection at different locations. The number of spots is decided by the convolution and pooling with a stride larger than one. Besides, such a process on the full image does not involve redundant convolution operations other than patch-wise pixel-labeling with window-sliding. While it only produces the output with very low resolution, it is called 'Naive Detection Net' and it needs to be improved. Refer to Fig. 3.4 for the result produced by the Naive Detection Network.

In addition to the resolution loss inherited from the classification net, the low localization accuracy is also caused by localization uncertainty of the classification net. For classifying

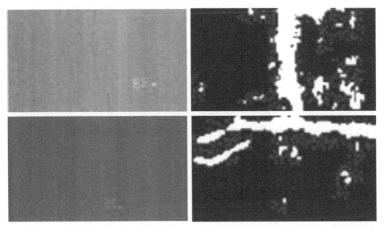

Fig. 3.4: Sample images and the outputs produced by Naive Detection Net. Left column: original image; right column: outputs of Naive Detection Net.

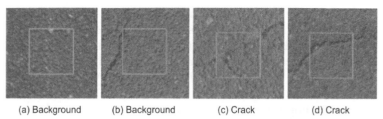

(a) Background   (b) Background   (c) Crack   (d) Crack

Fig. 3.5: Localization uncertainty of the classification network.

the image blocks, it is found that the network did a very good job when dealing with the blocks with a crack passing through the center of the blocks without cracks. However, they become ambiguous for the blocks with cracks near the border (*see* Fig. 3.5). It is called 'localization uncertainty', and if the localization uncertainty can be reduced, the detection performance improves.

In the early days of deep learning, researchers devoted substantial efforts to make the network converge, such as max pooling (Krizhevsky et al., 2012), dropout (Wan et al., 2013), increasing convolution/pooling stride (Krizhevsky et al., 2012), etc. Among them, the large strides significantly reduce the memory cost by cutting down on the output dimensions. However, it also discards a significant amount of information. In this part, the dilated convolution is implanted into the classification net to reduce the resolution loss without damage to the forward computing logic of the original classification network. As in Fig. 3.6, the network has two convolutional layers—the first layer conducts convolution on the input image with a kernel of 3×3 at stride 2; 'A', 'B', 'C' and 'D' denote that the outputs obtained by the convolutions operated at 'a', 'b', 'c' and 'd', respectively. Intuitively, with stride 2, the convolution will be conducted on locations centered with 'a' or 'b' or 'c' or 'd', depending on the starting point, and the output is shown in Fig. 3.6. While the direct way to eliminate coverage loss is by reducing the stride to 1; however, it involves additional outputs which break the output order (*see* Fig. 3.6). Obviously, we cannot continue the forward propagation with original kernels for a desired output. However, the messed outputs still have the information except for interpreting the additional values equal to the convolution results operated on the other starting points. In the next layer, if it interpolates 0s between each pair of elements of the original kernel and conducts the convolution operation

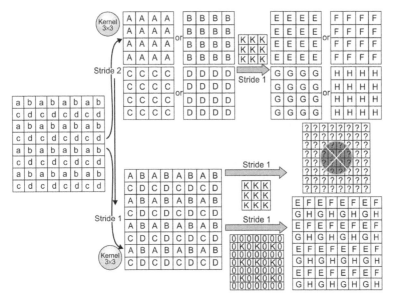

Fig. 3.6: Equivalent dilated convolution when stride changed.

at stride 1, the output is the same as the original convolution operation, but only with additional interpolated items. It turns out that the information is just the ones at the missed locations under the large-stride operations that will improve the resolution. Besides, the same idea can also be generalized to any pooling layers by picking up the elements at those sparsely located spots. In addition, once a stride reduction is applied to a specific layer, all the subsequent layers should take the dilated operation accordingly, and the dilation stride sizes have to accumulate along with each reduction from the previous layers. For example, assume there were three convolution layers in a network with stride sizes 2, 2 and 1, respectively. If the stride from first layer is reduced to 1, the dilation strides of second and third layers will be 2. If both first and second layer strides are reduced to 1, the dilation sizes of second and third layers have to be 2 and 4. As an exception, if the convolution kernel is 1×1 with stride 1, such as FC2 in the classification network, the dilation is not necessary.

Based on the analysis, we reduce the stride of MP2 to 1, set the dilation level of C3-C5 to 2, reduce the stride of C5 to 1, and set the stride of FC1 to 4 (note that we do not make change for

C1, C2, and MP1 because they have relatively small receptive fields which will make little difference). Finally, it will produce the output of 250×500-dimension. The dilated network will not improve the performance of network radically since it is only an equivalent implementation of the classification net. However, the experiments demonstrate that the increased output resolution is important for network convergence. Thus we conduct an end-to-end refining under larger field of view to reduce the localization uncertainty and improve the detection results. It is a fine-tuning strategy that will not retrain the parameters of C1-C5 which have acquired rich knowledge in the classification mode.

First, images of 400×400-pixel are used as the training data which is determined experimentally. As mentioned, training an end-to-end detection net with 1-pixel-width crack curve as GT is problematic due to the high risk of mismatch. We use the k-dilated GT image ('disk' structuring element was used for the dilation) (*see* Fig. 3.7). As long as the detected crack pixel falls in the dilated range of the 1-pixel GT, it will be treated as true positive, and the dilation size also indicates the uncertainty level.

Based on such settings, we implement FC2 with 3×3×1024 convolution layer and add another layer FC3 with kernels of size 1×1×3. Then it performs the fine-tuning with images of 400×400-pixel and GTs (note that the GTs are resized to 50×50 because there is an 8-time resolution loss from the first two layers). Besides, only crack and sealed crack images are involved because the background samples are taken into consideration automatically under FCN (Long et al., 2015). Figure 3.8 shows the detection results in Fig. 3.5. We see that refining reduces

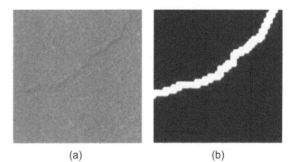

(a)   (b)

Fig. 3.7: Dilated GT. (a) An image block of 400×400 pixels; (b) dilated GT.

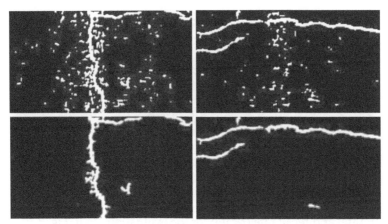

Fig. 3.8: Detection results of the images in Fig. 3.5. First row: outputs of the refined network; second row: final results after removing small noisy points.

the localization uncertainty and the false positives are in much smaller sizes which could be further removed by using simple denoising processes (Gonzalez et al., 2009).

3.5 Experiments

The data are obtained with a line-scan camera mounted on the top of a vehicle running at 100 km/h to scan 4.096-meter width road and produce an image of 2048×4096-pixel for every 2048 line-scans in 0.2048 seconds. Four hundred images from the industry are used for the experiments. The training-test ratio is 2:1.

Different from most object detection tasks (Everingham et al., 2017), Intersection Over Union (IOU) is not suitable for evaluating crack detection algorithms. Crack only occupies a very small area and the image consists mainly of background pixels (Tsai et al., 2010; Tsai and Chatterjee, 2017), and the precise pixel-level GTs are hard to obtain. It is infeasible to get accurate intersection area. As in Fig. 3.9, it is obvious that the detection result is very good; however, the IOU values for (b) and (c) are very low, at 0.13 and 0.2, respectively. Referred to Tsai and Chatterjee, 2017, we use Hausdorff Distance for overall evaluation of the crack localization accuracy. The metric is insensitive to foreground-background imbalance existing in most long-narrow object detection tasks. We also introduce region-based precision rate

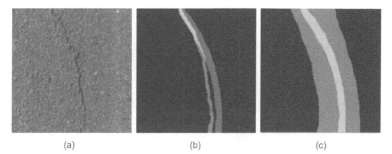

(a)   (b)   (c)

Fig. 3.9: Pixel-level mismatching: (a) a crack image; (b) detection result overlapped with the 3-width GT image; and (c) detection result overlapped with 12-width GT image. The transparent areas represent the n-dilated GT with different n.

(p-rate) and recall rate (r-rate) for the evaluation. As in Fig. 3.10, a crack image of 400×400-pixel is divided into small image patches (50×50-pixel). If a crack is detected in a patch, it is marked as '1s'. In the same way, for GT images, if there is a marked crack curve in a patch, it is a crack patch. Then the TP_{region}, FP_{region} and FN_{region} can be obtained by counting the square regions, and further used to calculate p-rate and r-rate: $P_{region} = \dfrac{TP_{region}}{TP_{region} + FP_{region}}$, $R_{region} = \dfrac{TP_{region}}{TP_{region} + FN_{region}}$. Then region-based F1 score ($F1_{region}$) can be computed as: $F1_{region} = \dfrac{2 * P_{region} * R_{region}}{P_{region} + R_{region}}$.

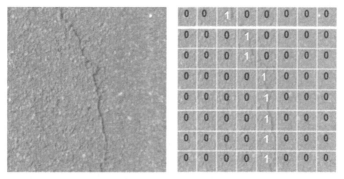

Fig. 3.10: Region-based evaluation. (a) Original crack image; (b) an illustration of counting crack and non-crack regions. The squares with label '1' are crack regions, and with label '0' are background regions.

We compare the method with the window-sliding-based method in terms of HD-score and computation efficiency. As shown in Table 3.2, method in Cha et al. (2017) is a region-based method and it cannot accurately locate the cracks, resulting in low HD-score and low p-rate. The time complexity is also high, which takes 10.2 seconds to process a full-size image. Instead, our method conducts forward computation only once for detection without introducing redundant convolutions, and it only takes 1.2 seconds and the localization accuracy is also very good.

Table 3.2: Performance comparison.

Method	p-rate	r-rate	HD-score	Time cost/s
Cha 2017	0.520	0.969	65	10.2
Ours	0.921	0.970	96	1.2

3.6 Summary

In this chapter, we discuss crack detection with FCN and dilated convolution. The method is much more efficient than window-sliding-based detection. The analysis also performed a brief study of an open problem: what is the difference between a DCNN-based classification network and detection/segmentation network? It indicated that the detection and segmentation network is a classification network working on a larger field of view with the receptive field as the input size (not considering the up-sampling/decoding layers).

4

Crack Detection with Generative Adversarial Learning

4.1 Background

In Chapter 3, we discussed an end-to-end crack detection network and developed an equivalent dense dilation layer for transfer learning which improved the crack localization accuracy. Actually, we found the training unstable, and the image size and dilation scale of the GTs used for the training were determined by trial and error. It was found that the network often 'converges' to the status that treats all pixels as background (BG), which can still achieve a very good loss. We named such a situation 'All Black' phenomenon. In this chapter, we propose a solution by introducing an asymmetric U-shape network and Crack-Patch-Only (CPO) supervised generative adversarial learning.

4.2 Generative Adversarial Networks

Generative adversarial network (GAN) (Goodfellow, 2014) is an important progress in deep learning. It proposes a novel learning strategy that can be used to train different models by conducting a max-min two-player game. The original GAN used two regular neural networks to play a contest in terms of data distribution: a generator, trained to map from a latent space to a distribution of interest and a discriminator, trained to distinguish between the data created by the generator and the data from the real distribution. Assume the generator is to learn a distribution p_g over data x, and a prior distribution on input noise $p_z(z)$. The mapping from noise to the data space is $G(z; \theta_g)$, where G is the function that represents the generator. Then, another neural network $D(x; \theta_d)$ gets a data with the same dimension as x and outputs a single scalar representing the probability of the real data rather than from a fake case. D and G are trained with the following value function $V(G, D)$:

$$\min_{G} \max_{D} V(D,G) = E_{x \sim p_{data}(x)} [log D(x)] + E_{z \sim p_z(z)} [log(1 - D(G(z)))]$$
(4.1)

It has been proved that by conducting the minmax game, the global goal of the optimization is $p_g = p_{data}$. An illustration of this theory can be found in Fig. 4.1 where the inputs are one-dimensional data with some distribution as indicated using the dash curve, the solid curve is the distribution of the generated data; it can be observed that the generated data distribution finally matches the real data distribution. While GAN is known to be difficult to train, Radford et al. (2016) proposed DC-GAN that uses convolution and de-convolution to build the generator, and it is trained to generate real-like images. The training is much easier and more stable under such a setting.

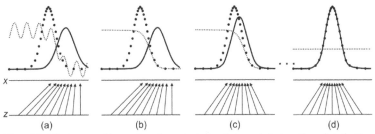

Fig. 4.1: The generative networks are trained to minimize the distribution difference between the real data and that from the generator (Fig. from reference, Goodfellow, 2014).

4.3 Deep Domain Adaptation

Domain adaptation is able to transfer two or multiple domains to a common domain. With the development of deep learning, deep domain adaptation was proposed where deep neural networks are trained for domain adaptation (Ganin, 2014). The most common context is that only one of the domains has a label while the data from other domains have no label but only domain information. The goal is to transform the data from the no-label domains into the labeled domain so that the influence of domain difference is minimized. As illustrated in Fig. 4.2, a neural network is served as the feature extractor which encodes an input image to a feature vector; a classifier at the top is used to predict class label while another classifier at the bottom is used to output a value representing how likely the data from the domain with label information is. The networks are trained with back-propagation; however, the main difference is that the domain classifier will send back the reversed gradient information to update the parameters. In that way, the data will be mapped to the space with the same domain. In this chapter, we use a pre-trained classifier to replace the discriminator in GAN for domain adaptation.

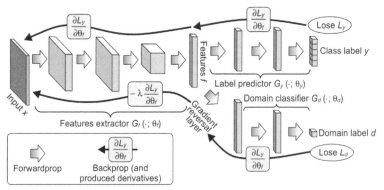

Fig. 4.2: Illustration of deep domain adaptation (Fig. from reference, Ganin, 2014).

4.3 Crack Detection with Generative Adversarial Learning

Figure 4.3 is an overview of the method with three characters: (1) CPO (Crack-Patch-Only) supervised generative adversarial leaning;

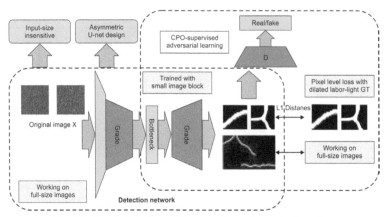

Fig. 4.3: Crack detection with generative adversarial learning.

(2) weak supervision with dilated GTs; and (3) asymmetric U-Net design. The CPO supervision and weak supervision with dilated GT provide the final objective function: $L_{final} = L_{adv} + L_{pixel}$. L_{adv} is the loss generated by the COP adversarial learning and L_{pixel} is the pixel-level loss obtained using the dilated GT images. The L_{adv} makes the network to generate crack images, and the L_{pixel} directs the network generate cracks at the expected locations. CPO supervision relies on the asymmetric U-Net.

As discussed in Chapter 3, directly training an FCN (Long, 2015), including U-Net (Ronneberger, 2015), for end-to-end per-pixel crack detection, cannot achieve the expected results. The reason is the data imbalance and unavailability of precise GTs. When conducting end-to-end training with FCN, the network will simply classify all the pixels as background and achieve quite 'good' accuracy (background pixels dominate the whole images). We named this phenomenon 'All Black' problem. Figure 4.4 shows that during training, the loss decreased rapidly and reached a very low value; however, the detection result of a crack image was all black as in Fig. 4.5. In order to solve such a problem, we added generative adversarial loss to the objective for training. The new loss forces the network to always generate crack-like detection result which overcomes the 'All Black' problem. DC-GAN (Radford, 2016) is employed. It is well known that the DC-GAN can generate real-like images from random noise by conducting the training with a max-min two-player game. Instead of directly

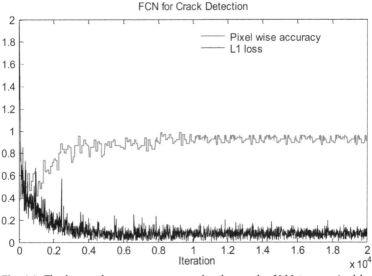

Fig. 4.4: The loss and accuracy curves under the regular U-Net supervised by labor-light (n-width) GTs.

applying the loss in reference (Goodfellow, 2014), it is better for G to maximize $\log(D(G(z)))$ instead of minimizing $\log(1 - D(G(z)))$. Therefore, the actual optimization strategy is to optimize the following two objectives alternatively:

$$\max_D V_D(D,G) = E_{x \sim p_d(x)} [logD(x)] + E_{z \sim p_d(z)} [log(1 - D(G(z)))] \tag{4.2}$$

$$\max_G V_G(D,G) = E_{z \sim p_d(z)} [log(D(G(z)))] \tag{4.3}$$

While our target is to force the network to produce crack-like images to realize the crack detection and overcome the 'All Black' issue, it only uses the crack GT patches as the real samples for adversarial training. The adversarial loss is $L_{adv} = -E_{x \in I} [logD(G(x))]$. Here, x is the input crack patch, I is the dataset of crack patches used to train the network, G is the asymmetric U-Net and D is the discriminator. The data of cack GT are augmented by manually marking 'crack-curve' images and pre-training a DC-GAN. The discriminator is reused to provide generative adversarial loss. Instead of generating full-size images, it trains the DC-GAN to

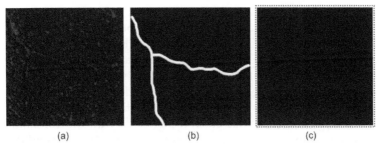

(a)   (b)   (c)

Fig. 4.5: 'All Black' problem encountered when using FCN based method for pixel-level crack detection on low-resolution images: (a) low-resolution image captured under industry setting; (b) n-width ground truth image and (c) detection result with 'well-trained' U-Net (*refer* Fig. 4.4).

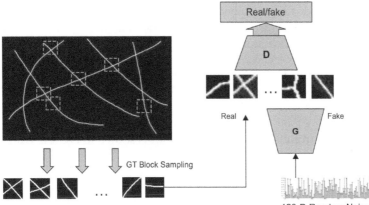

Fig. 4.6: Pre-train a rich pattern DC-GAN with augmented GT images based on CPO-supervision: the real GT dataset is augmented with manually marked 'crack' curve images to ensure the diversity of the crack patterns.

generate image patches using a large number of GT-like patches with rich crack patterns (*see* Fig. 4.6). Such a network is easy to train and can work on larger size images seamlessly.

The crack detection is formulated as a conditional image-generation problem. CPO-supervised adversarial learning is introduced to make the network generate GT-like crack patches. Notice that the discriminator only recognizes crack-GT patches as 'real' without considering the background patches. Normally, the discriminator should also treat 'all black' patches as real for the background (BG) translation. However, treating 'all black' patches as real will encourage the network to generate all black images as the detection results which cannot solve the 'All Black' issue. In order to include the translation of background samples, asymmetric U-Net architecture is used that takes a larger size crack image (256×256) to the asymmetric U-shape network while outputs a smaller size image (64×64) for end-to-end training. The larger input image has to be a crack image so that the correct output will always be a crack-like patch recognized by the discriminator as real. However, it includes the translation of both crack and BG samples (*see* Figs. 4.7 and 4.8).

To better understand how the asymmetric U-Net is able to include the BG translation ability by using only crack samples as the training data, we first performed a receptive field analysis under larger field of view. In Fig. 4.8, we assumed that there is a DCNN network, such as a classification network, with an $m{\times}m$ image patch as input, while the output is a single neuron representing the class label of the input image. When the same DCNN network is fed a larger input image (i.e., $M{\times}M$, $M{>}m$), it outputs multiple neurons (the number of neurons depends on the down-sampling rate of the DCNN), and each neuron represents a class label of the corresponding image patch of size $m{\times}m$ 'sampled' from the larger input image. As shown in Fig. 4.8, when

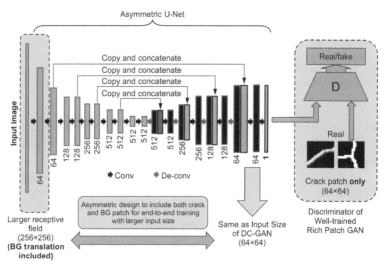

Fig. 4.7: Asymmetric U-Net under larger receptive field with CPO-supervision.

the network's input is an image of $m \times 3m$, the output consists of five neurons representing class labels of the five image patches, including both crack and non-crack samples. Indeed, with multi-layer fully convolutional network, each neuron actually has a receptive field with some specific size. Since the convolutional layer is input-size insensitive, operating the network under larger receptive field actually realized a multi-spot image sampling with the image size equal to the receptive field of the neuron. Thus, when performing an image translation, using a deep convolutional neural network with a larger input image, the process is equal to translating multiple smaller image samples at the same time. Based on the analysis, a crack image, larger than the input-size of the discriminator, was input into the asymmetric U-Net. It was then passed through the network to produce a down-sampled

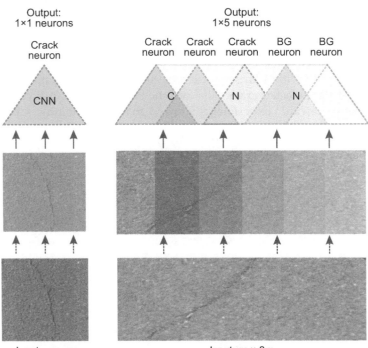

Fig. 4.8: With a larger input image, the CNN realizes multi-spot sampling with the same receptive field. In the right, the first three neurons represent three crack-samples while the last two are background neurons.

image to match the input-size of the discriminator, so that it can be used by the discriminator to produce the adversarial loss for generative adversarial learning. While the discriminator only treated crack-GT patch as real, it forces the network to generate crack patch as the detection result to prevent the 'All Black' issue. Since the network is trained to translate a larger crack image to a down-sampled crack image, it includes the translation of both crack and non-crack image patches. In this way, the network can be trained to translate both crack and background images for crack detection (*see* Fig. 4.9). Again, the training samples are composed of crack image patches only and without background image patches.

It introduced the CPO-supervised adversarial loss and the asymmetric U-Net to generate crack-GT patches. However, it is image-level supervision that does not specify where the crack should appear in the generated image. For crack detection, we need more information to know where the cracks are. As mentioned before, training an end-to-end crack detection network with 1-pixel crack curves as GTs is problematic. Instead, the dilated GTs with a larger crack area make the training possible and if the detected crack falls into the specified area, it gives a positive reward. Experiments showed that by combining CPO

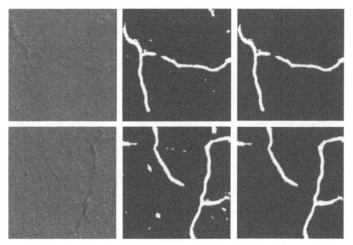

Fig. 4.9: Detection results of the final asymmetric U-Net. First column: low-resolution pavement image blocks; second column: the outputs of the network; third column: the final results after removing the isolated noise areas.

adversarial loss and the pixel loss with dilated GTs, the network can generate cracks at the expected locations. Specifically, we used 12-pixel-width crack GT to provide the weak supervision. The dilated GTs were obtained by dilating 1-pixel-width crack-GTs ('disk' structuring element was used for the dilation) and the weakly supervised pixel-level loss is $L_{pixel} = -E_{x \in I, y} [\|y - G(x)\|_1]$. Here, x is the input crack image patch, y is the dilated GT image, I is the dataset of larger size crack patches, G is the generator, and D is the discriminator. Overall, the final objective is: $L = L_{adv} + \lambda L_{pixel}$. The pixel loss is normalized during training, and λ can be determined via grid search. Once the training is finished, the discriminator is no longer needed and the generator itself can be used as the detection network.

Notice that the network is trained with small image blocks. However, under industry settings, the image size is much larger, such as pavement images with 2048×4096 pixels. A common solution to processing large image is to sample smaller image blocks from the full-size image and process them patch-by-patch (Cha, 2017) which is inefficient (Zhang, 2018). Since the asymmetric U-Net is designed as a fully convolutional network and the crack patterns are scale insensitive, it can work on arbitrarily larger images.

Figure 4.7 illustrates the architecture of the asymmetric U-Net. The convolutional kernel of the first layer is 7x7 with stride 2 followed by a rectified linear unit (ReLU) (Nair, 2010); then there is the 3x3 convolutional layer with stride 2 followed by a ReLU layer. They are the asymmetric part of U-Net which realizes a four-time down-sampling and reduces the input image to the same size as the output of the asymmetric U-Net. The remaining layers of the encoding and decoding parts are similar to regular U-Net (Ronneberger, 2015). After the last de-convolutional layer, another regular convolutional layer followed by a Tanh activation layer (LeCun, 2015) is used to translate the 64-channel feature maps to 1-channel image and it is compared with the dilated GT image for $L1$ loss computing. In summary, the network architecture is as follows, especially the encoding part:

C_64_7_2 - ReLU - C_64_3_2 - ReLU - C_128_3_1 - ReLU - C_128_3_2 - ReLU - C_256_3_1 - ReLU - C_256_3_2 - ReLU - C_512_3_1 - ReLU - C_512_3_2 - ReLU - C_512_3_1 - ReLU - C_512_3_2 - ReLU

The decoding part is:

DC_512_3_2 - ReLU - C_512_3_1 - ReLU - DC_256_3_2 - ReLU - C_256_3_1 - ReLU - DC_128_3_2 - ReLU - C_128_3_1 - ReLU - DC_64_3_1 - ReLU - C_64_3_1 - ReLU - C_1_3_1 - Tanh

Here, the naming rule follows 'layer type_channel number_kernel size_stride'. 'C' denotes convolution, 'DC' is de-convolution, and Tanh is the activation layer. For instance, 'C_64_7_2' means that the first layer is a convolutional layer, the number of channels is 64, the kernel size is 7, and the stride is 2.

The training is a two-stage strategy which employs transfer learning at two places. First, it pre-trains a DC-GAN. The DC-GAN is trained with the augmented GTs of 64×64-pixel to provide the adversarial loss for end-to-end training at the second stage. A total of 60,000 crack patches with various patterns are used. The cracks are dilated twice using a 'disk' structure with radius 3. The other training settings follow (Radford, 2016). Adam optimizer (Kingma, 2014) is used and the learning rate is 0.0002. The parameter for momentum updating is 0.9, batch size is 128, and the input 'noise' is 128 dimensions. A total of 100 epochs (each epoch is total images/batch size = 60000/128 iterations) are run to obtain the final model. Then the well-trained discriminator was concatenated to the end of the asymmetric U-Net to provide the adversarial loss at the second stage.

Inspired by Zhang et al. (2018), it also pre-trains the encoding part of the generator under the classification setting. Figure 4.10 shows the low-level feature maps of a classification network trained with crack and non-crack patches. The training samples are crack and non-crack patches. The network extracted the same crack pattern as the original image which means that the network is able to learn useful information with weakly supervised information, such as crack/non-crack image label. The parameters of the well-trained network are used to initialize the encoding part of the generator, and the other settings are similar to original DC-GAN, except the replacing generator with the asymmetric U-Net and setting the objective function with Eq. 4.7.

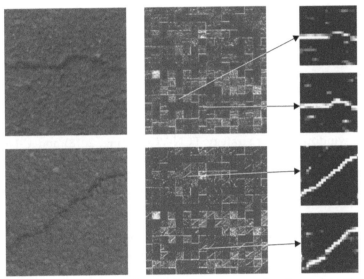

Fig. 4.10: Weakly supervised learning is able to learn crack pattern information. Left side: image blocks sent to the classification network; middle: feature maps after the first convolutional layer; right side: feature maps with the similar crack patterns to the original image blocks.

4.4 Experiments

We make comparisons with six crack detection methods on two crack datasets: CFD (Shi, 2016) captured with a cellphone while the data collected using a line-scan camera from industry. CFD dataset is a public dataset with hand-labeled GTs. The dataset has 118 pavement crack images of 320×480-pixel. The images were captured by people standing on the road and holding an iPhone near the road, and the pixel-level GTs are manually marked. As mentioned in the last chapter, the industrial crack images are often with thin cracks which are difficult to precisely mark the GTs at pixel-level. The GTs are marked using 1-pixel curves. Such GTs may not match the true crack locations at pixel-level, and processing of such images is more challenging. In the same way, region-based p-rate, r-rate, and HD-score are used as the metrics for the evaluation. CrackIT-v1 (Oliveira, 2014), MFCD (Li, 2018),

CrackForest (Shi, 2016), method in reference (Cha, 2017), FCN-VGG (Yang, 2018), and U-Net (Ronneberger, 2015) are the methods for comparison. CrackIT and MFCD are state-of-the-art methods, using traditional image processing techniques. CrackForest is state-of-the-art machine learning method before deep learning. Method in reference (Cha, 2017), FCN-VGG (Yang, 2018), and U-Net (Ronneberger, 2015) are deep learning methods. Method in reference (Cha, 2017) is a block-level detection approach based on window-sliding strategy. FCN-VGG (Yang, 2018) and U-Net are trained with carefully marked pixel-level GTs which is labor-intensive. Figure 4.11 and Table 4.1 are the results on CFD, and Fig. 4.12 and Table 4.2 are the results on industry data. It shows that CrackIT missed most crack pixels and cannot even detect any cracks in the second and third images in Fig. 4.11 where the cracks are thin. It also failed to detect cracks from the images in Fig. 4.12. For MFCD, it has a good detection ability and can detect most of the cracks on both CFD and industry data; however, it did not solve the noise problem well and achieved low precision rates and HD-score. CrackForest can identify most of the cracks and achieve good recall on both datasets. However, it is not good at noise removal on the industry images due to the complicated pavement textures. For method in reference (Cha, 2017), it only produces image block labels and obtains low p-rates on both datasets. FCN-VGG and U-Net (Ronneberger, 2015) perform well on CFD since the precisely marked GTs were available for the end-to-end training. However, they encountered the 'All Black' issue when dealing with pavement images from industry due to data imbalance and unavailability of precise pixel-level GTs. Our method, CrackGAN, overcame the 'All Black' problem and achieved a very good performance on both CFD and the industrial data.

In addition to accuracy, the computation efficiency is also compared. The average processing time for an image of 2048×4096-pixel is shown in Table 4.3. The three methods are conducted with Matlab 2016b on HP 620 workstation with 32G memory and twelve i7 cores. For deep learning methods, they are conducted on the same computer but running on the NVIDIA 1080Ti GPU with Pytorch. CrackGAN takes less time than U-Net because it cuts off the last couple of de-convolutional layers for the asymmetric design.

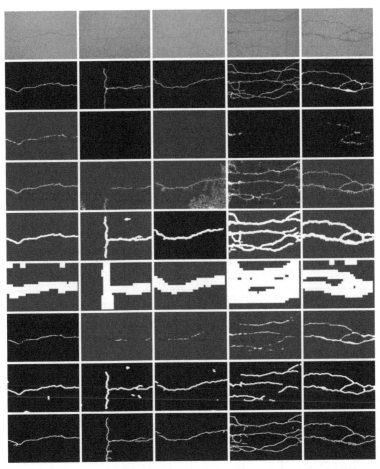

Fig. 4.11: Comparison of detection results on CFD dataset using different methods. From top to bottom: original images, GT images and the detection results of CrackIT, MFCD, CrackForest, Cha, 2017, FCN-VGG, U-Net and CrackGAN (proposed).

In addition to the pavement crack detection, using public dataset CFD and the low-resolution images from industry, the proposed method is also good to handle other crack detection problems. Figure 4.13 provides the detection results on datasets (Yang, 2018) that contain concrete pavement images and concrete wall images.

Table 4.1: Quantitative comparison on CFD dataset.

Methods	p-rate	r-rate	F_1-score	HD-score
CrackIT	88.02%	45.11%	59.65%	21
MFCD	80.90%	87.47%	84.01%	85
CrackForest	85.31%	90.22%	87.69%	88
Cha 2017	68.97%	98.21%	81.03%	70
FCN	86.01%	92.30%	89.04%	88
U-Net	88.01%	90.02%	89.01%	90
CrackGAN	89.21%	96.01%	91.28%	95

Table 4.2: Quantitative comparison on industrial dataset.

Methods	p-rate	r-rate	F_1-score	HD-score
CrackIT	89.10%	2.52%	4.90%	9
MFCD	50.90%	87.47%	64.35%	67
CrackForest	31.10%	98.01%	47.22%	63
Cha 2017	69.20%	98.30%	81.22%	64
FCN-VGG [49]	0.00%	0.00%	N/A	N/A
U-Net	0.00%	0.00%	N/A	N/A
CrackGAN	89.21%	96.01%	91.28%	95

Table 4.3: Comparison of computation efficiency.

Method	Time	Method	Time
CrackIT	6.1 s	FCN	2.8 s
MFCD	5.2 s	U-Net	2.2 s
CrackForest	4.0 s	CrackGAN	1.6 s
Cha 2017	10.2 s		

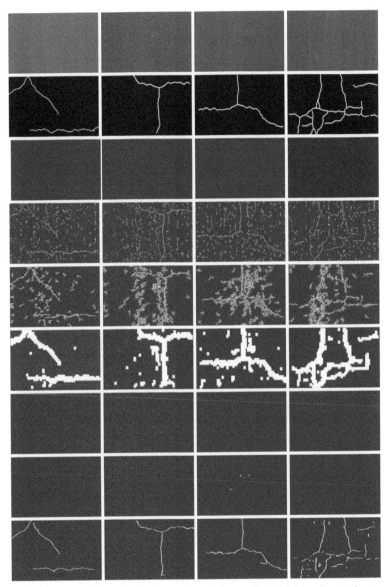

Fig. 4.12: Comparison of detection results on low-resolution dataset from industry using different methods. From top to bottom: original image, ground truth images and the detection results of CrackIT, MFCD, CrackForest, Cha, 2017, FCN-VGG ('All Black'), U-Net ('All Black') and CrackGAN, respectively.

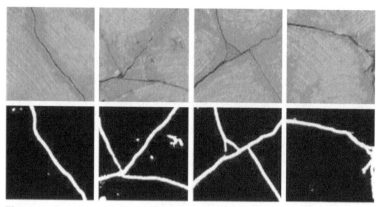

Fig. 4.13: Detection results on concrete wall and concrete pavement images. First row: original concrete wall images. Second row: corresponding results of CrackGAN. Third row: original concrete pavement images. Fourth row: the corresponding results of CrackGAN.

4.5 Summary

In this chapter, we discussed deep generative adversarial network for crack detection. The method solves an important issue, the 'All Black' problem, existing in deep learning-based pixel-level crack detection. An asymmetric U-Net architecture is proposed and a CPO supervised generative adversarial learning strategy is used to generate expected crack patterns and implicitly enables both crack and background image translation abilities. The work solved an important problem—data imbalance in object detection.

5

Self-Supervised Structure Learning for Crack Detection

5.1 Background

We discussed crack detection with supervised deep learning from Chapter 1 to Chapter 4. These methods, as discussed, rely on a reasonable amount of paired training data obtained by making non-trivial GTs manually, which is expensive, especially for pixel-level annotations. Since the model cannot handle crack detection with different backgrounds, the actual workload is quite heavy because we need to re-mark the GTs and re-train the model for the new detection task. Thus, it is worthwhile to rethink the automatic crack detection by taking into account the labor cost. As a pre-exploration of the future Artificial Intelligence object detection system, in this chapter, we discuss a self-supervised structure learning network that can be trained without using paired data. The target is achieved by training an additional reverse network to translate the output back to the input simultaneously. First, a labor-free structure library is prepared and set as the target domain for structure learning. Then a dual network is built with two GANs: one is trained to translate a crack image patch X to a structural patch Y, and the other is trained to translate Y back to X, simultaneously. The experiments demonstrate that with such settings, the network can be trained to translate a crack image to the GT-like image with similar structure patterns for use in crack detection. The proposed approach is validated on four crack datasets and achieves comparable performance with that of the state-of-the-art supervised approaches.

5.2 Image-to-image Translation GAN

Original GAN is with a generator made with fully connected layers. While the original GAN is difficult to train, Radford et al. (2016) proposed the DC-GAN which replaced the fully connected layers with convolutional layers; and the network was trained to optimize the convolutional kernels to generate real-like images where training became much easier. In order to make GAN more controllable, Mirza and Osindero (2014) proposed conditional GAN which added additional information in the input to generate specific output according to the condition. Based on conditional GAN and DC-GAN, Isola et al. (2017) set up the condition with an input image and the network became an image-to-image translation network trained with paired images. The work broadened the application of supervised GAN. Zhu et al. (2017) proposed cycle-consistent adversarial networks that could be trained without using paired data for image style transfer. Based on these works, we formulated crack detection as an image-to-image translation problem, and introduced the cycle-consisting adversarial learning to train the networks without manually labeling GTs (*see* Fig. 5.1 for an illustration of different GANs).

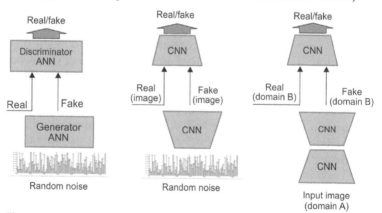

Fig. 5.1: Architectures of different GANs: (a) Original GAN; (b) DC-GAN; (c) image-to-image translation GAN.

5.3 Structure Learning

Structure learning tries to learn the mapping function between inputs and structure patterns that can represent the inputs used to address computer vision problems. For example, Kontschieder et al. (2011) utilized structure learning to assist semantic image labeling; Dollár et al. (2013) employed structure learning for edge/contour detection. Since cracks exhibit strong structural patterns, such as straight lines, cross shapes, T-junctions, Y-junctions, etc., structure learning is also used for crack detection (Dollár, 2013). For example, Shi et al. (2016) introduced structure learning for crack detection where a random decision forest is trained to map the crack patch to a structure patch. The works trained a cluster to group the structure patches into a limited number of representative patterns, and with the paired image-GT data, a random forest was trained to find the mapping relationship from input images to the structure patches. Different from these works, we used the cycle-consistent generative adversarial learning to find the source-target mapping relationship between two domains automatically, and the target domain (structure library) is obtained without manually marking GTs based on a self-supervised strategy.

Instead of spending a lot of time on preparing GTs, unsupervised/self-supervised learning has been receiving increasing attention in recent years. While there is no clear line between unsupervised learning and self-supervised learning, two main settings are used in existing self-supervised learning: one is to learn features using an unsupervised pre-text task, and then apply the learned knowledge to other tasks (Doersch, 2017) and the other is to introduce external data and relate the images to the introduced data to supervise the training. Doersch et al. (2017) used the similarity measurements among randomly cropped image patches to supervise the learning for context prediction; Noroozi et al. (2016) trained a CNN to solve jigsaw puzzle problem to provide self-supervision, and the real task was to learn visual representations. Sohn et al. (2017) introduced unsupervised domain adaptation for face recognition from unlabeled video frames, where still labeled images were used to pre-train the network. We use a dual network to translate the output back to the input for self-supervision; and as an assistant factor, a labor-free structure library is introduced for structure learning which helps the forward network generate consistent structure patterns as the original cracks for detection.

5.4 Crack Detection with Cycle-GAN

We try to build an image-to-image translation network that can translate crack image to GT-like image with similar structure pattern, using structured curves to represent cracks. Two separate datasets/domains are used to train the network: a crack-image set X and a structure library Y with images $\{x_i\}$ and $\{y_i\}$, respectively. In Fig. 5.2, the network consists of two image-to-image translation GANs: a forward GAN F translates images from X to Y ($F: X \rightarrow Y$), and a reverse GAN R translates image from Y to X ($R: Y \rightarrow X$). Two discriminators, D_x and D_y are introduced: D_x aims to distinguish between images $\{x_i\}$ and the translated images $\{R(y_i)\}$ with forward adversarial loss L_{advf}; and D_y aims to distinguish between $\{y_i\}$ and $\{F(y_i)\}$ with reverse adversarial loss L_{advr}. D_y is designed as a pre-trained deeper discriminator working under a larger field of view to succeed the training. Two cycle-consistent losses with L1-distance are used in the forward GAN denoted as $L1_{fc}$ and in the reverse GAN, denoted as $L1_{rc}$. Overall, the objective function is:

$$L = (L_{advf} + L_{advr}) + \lambda(L1_{fc} + L1_{rc}) \tag{5.1}$$

where λ can be determined by grid search. In addition, the networks are designed as fully convolutional networks trained with small image patches; however, they can process images of arbitrary size.

The training data consist of two parts: the crack patches and structure library. The structure library contains a large number of binary image patches of various structure patterns; and the crack patches are prepared by cropping crack blocks of 64×64 randomly from the full-size crack images according to reference (Zhang, 2018). Different from other learning-based detection approaches (Shi, 2016; Yang, 2018), no manually marked GTs were involved. Instead, a labor-free structure library is employed to assist training. First, a GT-like dataset is made by collecting data from the public datasets. Here, the object boundary annotations of VOC object detection dataset (Everingham, 2017), object contour annotations of Berkeley segmentation dataset (Martin, 2001), and GTs of public crack detection datasets (Zou, 2012; Yang, 2018) are used.

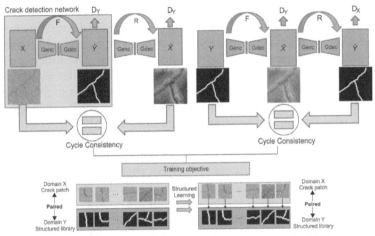

Fig. 5.2: Overview of the proposed approach with cycle-GAN.

As shown in Fig. 5.3, the annotations are the curves representing boundaries of objects or cracks; the structure library consists of image patches of 64×64 sampled from the annotations. Then data are further augmented, using image rotation and distortion, and the structure patches are dilated by using a disk structure with radius equal to 3.

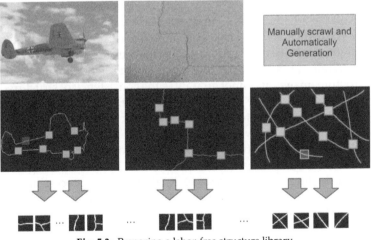

Fig. 5.3: Preparing a labor-free structure library.

As seen in Fig. 5.2, a dual-network is introduced and the training is performed by checking the consistency of both forward and backward cycles. The objective function contains two parts: the adversarial loss and the cycle consistency loss. The adversarial loss helps the detection network to generate GT-like structure images, and the cycle consistency loss makes sure that the generated structure patterns are consistent with the input cracks. It is well known that by conducting a max-min two-player game, the generative adversarial network can be trained to generate real-like images even from noise. In practice, it is realized by optimizing the following two objectives alternatively (Tran, 2017). In our case, the generator is an encoding/decoding U-shaped network that inputs an image and generates another image (as the fake image). Here z is a crack patch from the training data which serves as the input condition that makes the generator produce a specific image related to the input, and x is the image from the structure library as the real sample. In the same way, the reverse network translates a structured image, including the generated structured image by the forward network, to a crack patch for adversarial learning. The adversarial loss can help the generator to create structure images by requiring the outputs to have identical distribution as the training data. However, the structure library may have different distribution from the expected GTs in terms of the structure patterns. Thus, different from the original cycle-GAN, the adversarial loss of the forward GAN is provided by a pre-trained DC-GAN whose discriminator is fully copied and the weights are reused to serve as a domain adaptor.

While the adversarial loss can help the generator to create structure images, it cannot guarantee the consistency of structured patterns between the output and the input. The adversarial loss alone is inadequate for translating a crack patch to the desired structure patch and vice versa. However, researchers found that by introducing an extra cycle-consistency constraint, the network can be trained to realize the goal (Zhu, 2017). As in Fig. 5.2, for each sample, x from dataset X, after a cycle processing, the network should be able to bring x back to the original patch, i.e., $x \rightarrow G(x) \rightarrow F(G(x)) \sim x$. In the same way, for each structure image y from the structure library Y, after a cycle of processing, the network is also able to bring y back to the original image, i.e.,

$y \rightarrow R(y) \rightarrow F(R(y)) \sim y$. Such constraint can be formulated to have the following cycle-consistency loss:

$$L_{cyc}(F,R) = E_{x \sim p_d(x)} [\|R(F(x)) - x\|_1] + E_{y \sim p_d(y)} [\|F(R(y)) - y\|_1 \quad (5.2)$$

The entire network includes two image-to-image translation GANs: a forward GAN F that inputs a crack image and generates a structured image; and a reverse GAN R that inputs a structured image and generates a crack image. F and R use the same network architecture where each GAN includes two parts: the generator and discriminator. The generator is a U-shape (Ronneberger, 2015) image-to-image translation network and the discriminator is a classification network with a larger receptive field that is realized by adding another stride convolution layer to the original discriminator, named deeper discriminator.

As shown in Fig. 5.4, the U-Net includes three components: encoding layers, decoding layers, and skipping layers. The encoder consists of four repeated convolution layers with 3x3 kernels; after each of the first three convolutional layers, the number of feature map channels doubles. For the decoder, it consists of four 3x3 deconvolution layers that 'up-sample' the feature maps; the input of each deconvolution layer is the output of the last layer and the skipping layers from the encoding part. Each convolution or deconvolution layer is followed by a ReLU layer (Nair, 2010). After the last deconvolution layer, another regular convolution layer with 3x3 kernels is configured to translate the 128-channel

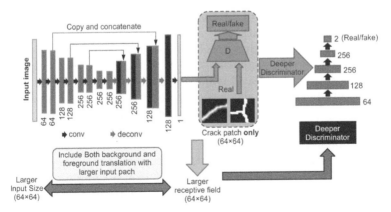

Fig. 5.4: Network architecture of the forward GAN.

feature maps to the output image, and it is compared with the dilated GT for $L1$ loss computation. In summary, the architecture of the generator is as follows:

The encoding part:

C_64_3_2 - ReLU - C_64_3_1 - ReLU - C_128_3_2 - ReLU - C_128_3_1 - ReLU - C_256_3_2 - ReLU - C_256_3_1 - ReLU - C_256_3_2 - ReLU - C_256_4_1 - ReLU

The decoding part:

DC_256_3_2 - ReLU - DC_256_3_2 - ReLU - DC_128_3_2 - ReLU - DC_128_3_2 - ReLU - C_1_3_1

The naming rule follows the format 'layer type_kernel number_kernel size_stride'; 'C' denotes convolution and 'DC' is deconvolution. For instance, 'C_64_3_2' means that the first layer is a convolution layer, the number of kernels is 64, the kernel size is 3 and the stride is 2.

We use a network architecture named 'deeper discriminator', and discuss the difference from the original image-to-image translation GANs (Isola, 2017). In convolutional GAN, a generator is usually configured with a series of deconvolution layers to generate images from random noise, and the discriminator is set up with a classifier to discriminate the generated image and real image. With such a setting, the discriminator can only process image patches with the same size as the generator's outputs. Isola et al. (2017) configured the generator and discriminator with fully convolutional networks where the input can be of arbitrary size. However, when it inputs a larger size image, the output of the discriminator will have multiple labels, which indeed do not change the input size of each sample, i.e., the receptive field of each output neuron/label is the same. For example, in Fig. 5.5, originally the discriminator is designed to discriminate a patch of $m{\times}m$ as real or fake. With such a setting, when the generator is fed in a real crack image patch with larger size, $2m{\times}2m$, the discriminator will output a $2{\times}2$ label matrix where each label corresponds to an image sample of $m{\times}m$ from the larger input image. As illustrated in Fig. 5.5, the image samples include two different types of images: the image patch containing a crack pattern or the 'All Black' patch. They are both considered as real images since they are all sampled from the real larger

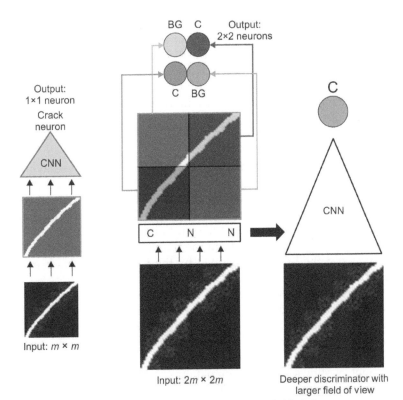

Fig. 5.5: Deeper discriminator with larger field of view.

structure images. It has been discussed that the crack-like object detection suffers from serious data imbalance problem because the background usually dominates the image area. Treating both crack patch and 'All Black' patch as real can weaken the foreground-background distinguishing ability and fail the task. Here, we use a discriminator that takes a larger size image as input but treats it as a single image for discrimination, i.e., each larger input corresponds to a single label. The benefit of such a design is that the discriminator will only treat the structured patch (crack patch) as real and force the generator to pay more attention to the crack areas in a larger input image to avoid background area dominating the training samples, and overcome the data imbalance. It is realized by explicitly adding a stride convolution layer to the discriminator; then the discriminator will output a single label/neuron for each input image, named deeper discriminator. In detail, the discriminator consists of five 3×3 convolution layers and a fully connected layer followed by a Softmax layer with 2-channel output representing the class label of a 64×64 image. In brief, the discriminator is:

C_64_3_2 - ReLU - C_128_3_2 - ReLU - C_256_3_2 - ReLU - C_256_3_2 - ReLU - FC_4_2 -SM

The 'FC' is fully connected layer and 'SM' is Softmax layer; and they together serve as a classifier to determine if the input image is real, and to provide the adversarial loss. For the reverse network, it uses the same architecture where the input is a structure patch and the output is a real-like crack image with background textures. The crack images from the training data are considered as real and the images generated by the U-shape generator are considered as fake.

Generic knowledge learned from large-scale data, such as ImageNet (Deng, 2009) can be used to extract crack pattern and it is also beneficial in network training, as shown in Fig. 5.6. As has been discussed in Chapter 4, the output after conducting convolution using a pertained image classification network on ImageNet shows strong crack patterns in the original crack. We adopt the same routine and initialize parameters of the forward generator using a pre-trained model. In addition, different from the original cycle-GAN, it also pre-trains a DC-GAN with the structure library, as discussed in Chapter 4. The discriminator of the well-trained DC-GAN is transferred and concatenated to the end of the generator in the forward GAN to provide generative adversarial loss and update the parameters via backpropagation. The pre-trained discriminator indeed serves as a domain adaptor that forces the generated image to become a structured patch. For the discriminator in the reverse GAN, it is trained from scratch. In addition, it is worth mentioning that we tried to train the original cycle-GAN directly without pre-training a DC-GAN. However, it is difficult to achieve satisfactory results. We know GAN is trained by reducing the distribution difference between the generated images and the real data. For a specific dataset, the expected detection results/GTs could have different distribution with the structure library concerning the crack patterns, with the

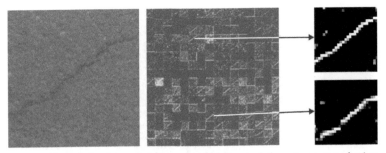

Fig. 5.6: Knowledge learned from a classification task has strong transferring ability and can be used for parameter initialization to ease the training on different tasks.

belief that the generative loss will tend to make the generated images have the same distribution as the structure library. That is not the truth and will give the generator false information for updating the parameters, and increase the failure possibility. That could be the reason for the failure.

After initialization, the parameters of the generators and the discriminator in the reverse GAN are updated alternatively. When the Adam (Kingma, 2014) optimizer is used, the learning rate is 0.0002 and the parameter for updating the momentum is 0.9. Since the two cycles are trained simultaneously, and the cycle-consistency restriction is applied to both forward and reverse GANs, the training samples include both real crack patches and generated crack patches, and the structure patches from the library and the generated structure patches. Thus, an additional buffer is needed to store the generated images during the training, and so 50 previously generated images are stored. The batch size is 6 due to memory limitation. A total of 100 epochs were run and the model parameters are saved every five epochs. In this way, the networks can be trained to generate similar structure patterns according to the input cracks. The forward GAN is trained to translate the original crack patches to the structured patches, and the reverse GAN is trained to translate the structured patches to crack images. Refer to Fig. 5.7 for the results of such translation on the test set. In the experiment, the validation results are saved every twenty-iterations to monitor the training. Finally, all the saved models are tested to select the best one as the detection network. After the training, the reverse GAN and the discriminator

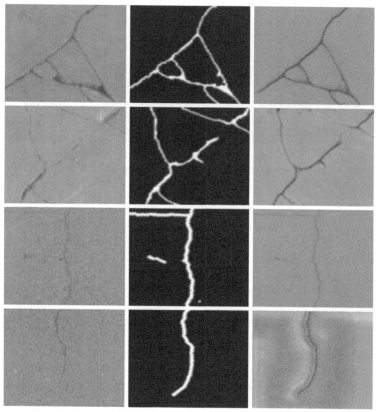

Fig. 5.7: Results from the image-to-image translation network. Left column: the test images from references (Yang, 2018; Zou, 2012).

of the forward GAN are no longer used, and the generator of the forward GAN alone serves as the detection network to translate a pavement image into the GT-like image for crack detection.

5.4 Experiments

The experiments are conducted with an HP workstation with Intel i7 CPU and 32G memory. An Nvidia 1080Ti GPU was configured and *PyTorch* was used to perform the training and testing. The proposed method is compared with seven crack detection methods on two representative datasets: the public dataset CFD (Shi, 2016) captured with a cellphone and the data from industry.

As mentioned in Chapter 4, the industrial data have no precisely marked pixel-level GTs since the crack width is tiny and the boundary is vague. The GTs are marked by using 1-pixel curves which are used for crack/non-crack block sampling. Another two datasets are also employed: CrackTree dataset (Zou, 2012) and FCN dataset (Yang, 2018). CrackTree is a pavement crack detection dataset with 206 pavement images of 600×800-pixel. The accurate GTs are also available. FCN dataset is also a public dataset composed of 800 images. The images are collected from multiple sources, including historical crack images from internet, newly captured crack images of concrete walls from buildings, and the pavement crack images. While the multi-source images are taken at different distances with different cameras, the resolution levels range from 72 dpi to 300 dpi. The GTs are manually marked at pixel-level. For evaluation, the region-based p-rate, r-rate, and HD-score are used. Since the proposed approach is a self-supervised/unsupervised method, it is compared with the rule-based approaches, which could be viewed as unsupervised methods and machine learning-based methods. The rule-based approaches are CrackIT (Oliveira, 2014) and MFCD (Li, 2018), and the machine learning methods are CrackForest (Shi, 2016) and CrackGAN as seen in Chapter 4.

The sample images with the detection results and the quantitative measurements in terms of precision, recall, F-measure and Hausdorff score are presented in Fig. 5.8 and Table 5.1, respectively. It can be observed that CrackIT can detect the clear cracks with distinct crack width, such as the cracks in the first image, but it misses most thin cracks in the second and third images. MFCD shows strong crack-detection ability and can detect most cracks. However, it may introduce noise when dealing with images having non-smooth background. CrackForest achieves very good results with data published in the paper. CrackGAN achieves the best performance.

The detection results on industrial dataset are present in Table 5.2 and Fig. 5.9. Different from CFD data, there is no precise pixel-level GTs for this dataset. The 1-pixel GTs are not suitable for end-to-end training, and it will easily run into the 'All Black' local minimal due to the pixel-level mismatching and data imbalance. Therefore, the results of end-to-end training are the ones trained by using the mixed datasets of CFD, CrackTree and FCN when

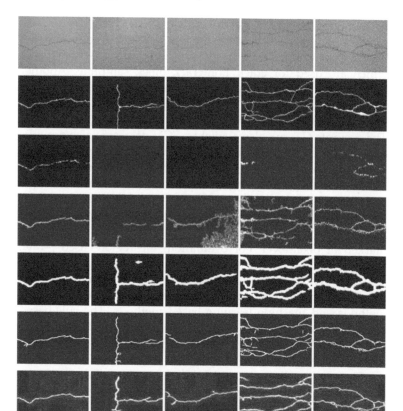

Fig. 5.8: Comparison of detection results on CFD data. From top to bottom: original image, GTs, and the detection results of CrackIT, MFCD, CrackForest, CrackGAN and the proposed method, respectively.

Table 5.1: Quantitative comparison on CFD data.

Method	*p*-rate	*r*-rate	*F1*-score	*HD*-score
CrackIT	88.02%	45.11%	59.65%	21
MFCD	80.90%	87.47%	84.01%	85
CrackForest	85.31%	90.22%	87.69%	88
CrackGAN	88.03%	96.11%	91.88%	96
Proposed	88.01%	93.02%	89.01%	92

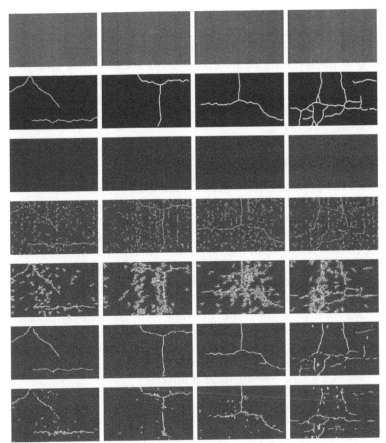

Fig. 5.9: Comparison of detection results on industrial data. From top to bottom: original image, GTs, and the detection results of CrackIT, MFCD, CrackForest, CrackGAN and the proposed method, respectively.

Table 5.2: Quantitative evaluation on industrial data.

Method	*p*-rate	*r*-rate	*F1*-score	*HD*-score
CrackIT	89.10%	2.52%	4.90%	9
MFCD	50.90%	87.47%	64.35%	67
CrackForest	31.10%	98.01%	47.22%	63
CrackGAN	89.21%	96.01%	91.28%	95
Proposed	78.01%	86.02%	80.01%	78

the pixel-level GTs are given. As shown in Fig. 5.9, CrackIT shows similar results using CFD data, and most cracks are missed. MFCD detects most cracks but also introduces many noises due to the complicated pavement texture. CrackGAN achieved best results because of the supervised end-to-end training. The proposed method trained with the assistance of the structure library achieved comparable results with CrackGAN without labor-expensive GTs.

5.5 Ablation Study

GAN has been proved to perform the learning via reducing the distribution difference between real data and generated data. As reported in reference (Zhu, 2017), the distribution consistency could be any permutation of the images which cannot guarantee the consistency of input-output patterns. In Fig. 5.10, the images on the bottom row are the generated image patches trained without cycle-consistency loss while the top row are image patches with both the adversarial loss and the cycle-consistency loss. Without cycle-consistency loss, the network can generate structured image patches. However, the generated structure patterns are quite random and do not match the input crack patterns well, and cannot be used for crack detection. Notice that the testing is conducted on the training dataset directly.

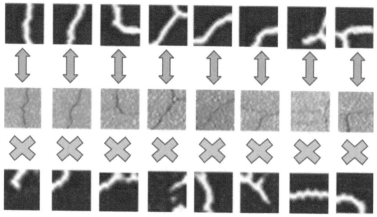

Fig. 5.10: Testing results on training set with and without cycle consistent loss. Top row: generated images with the proposed setting, and bottom row: generated images without cycle consistent loss.

One of the main differences from the original GAN is the modified discriminator which works with a larger input image (larger than the receptive field of the generator). The discriminator would treat both the structured patch and the 'All Black' patches as real where the structured patches represent the crack patches and the 'All Black' patches represent the background patches, respectively. From Fig. 5.11, it can be observed that without deeper discriminator, the network cannot generate expected results but can only produce some nonsensical textures. A

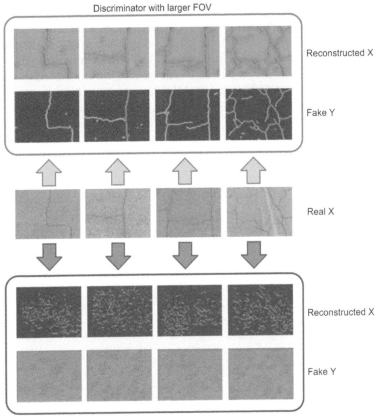

Fig. 5.11: Experiments with and without deeper discriminator. Images at the top: the proposed setting and images on the bottom: results with the original cycle-GAN.

possible explanation is that when the discriminator treated both structured patch and 'All Black' patch as real, its function was greatly weakened. In contrast, the network trained with deeper discriminator can handle the problem properly.

5.6 Summary

In this chapter, we discussed a self-supervised structure learning approach for crack detection without relying on manually marked GTs. The method has the potential to realize the real fully automatic crack detection that does not need to manually mark GTs for training. We formulate crack detection as an unsupervised structure learning problem by introducing a labor-free structure library to assist the training of cycle-GAN. A discriminator with a larger field of view was used as it only treated the crack patches as real, and the data imbalance problem is overcome. Moreover, we combine domain adaptation and generative adversarial networks to handle object detection, which is a general means that can be applied to other computer vision problems.

6

Deep Edge Computing

6.1 Background

We have discussed the algorithms which solved the crack detection problem with deep neural networks. For the training and deployment of deep neural networks, GPUs and TPUs were the primary hardware because of their strong computational ability. However, most applications require to deploy the system on the edge with limited computational resources, e.g., mobile phones and embedded systems. In this chapter, we discuss soft technologies of deep edge computing to facilitate the deployment of deep learning models, including parameter pruning, knowledge distillation, and model quantization for constructing lightweight networks.

6.2 Model Pruning

Model pruning done is to reduce the computational complexity by model parameters pruning. A common approach is to directly set part of the parameters to zero. According to the distribution of the parameters set to zero, model pruning can be structural pruning and unstructured pruning. For unstructured pruning, the parameters are pruned according to some formula and the pruned parameter distribution looks random. Such unstructured pruning leads to irregular, sparse weight matrices, which rely on indices to be stored in a compressed format. As a result, they are less compatible with parallel computing mechanism in GPUs and multicore CPUs. Figure 6.1 is an example of unstructured pruning.

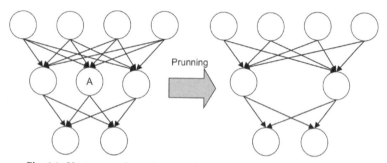

Fig. 6.1: Unstructured pruning; weights related to neuron A are removed.

How to select the weight to be pruned is the core of unstructured pruning. The first unstructured model pruning method is the optimal brain damage (OBD) (LeCun et al., 1989). The method uses Hessian matrix to represent the optimization objective, that is, to minimize the difference in loss function before and after model pruning. Schraudolph et al. (2014) proposed to replace Hessian matrix with General Gauss Newton approximation to solve the calculation complexity problem. However, with the occurrence of 'early stop', the gradient of parameters no longer ends with zero. For 'early stop' model, Laurent et al. (2020) proposed a pruning method that performed the optimization by tuning the parameters in a small range. The methods to control the variation range of parameters include multi-step optimization (Zeng and Urtasun, 2018; Wang et al., 2019), and regularization-based method (Nocedal and Wright, 2000). Magnitude pruning (MP) (Han et al., 2015) is another method to evaluate the importance of parameters for the pruning.

After parameter pruning, indices are used to represent weight matrices in the sparse format, thereby achieving storage reduction. A representative sparse representation format is the Compressed Sparse Row (CSR) format (Ma et al., 2021). CSR format represents a matrix using three arrays: nonzero weight values, column indices, and the extents of rows. The row pointer represents the index of the first non-zero value in each row. This representation requires $2n + r + 1$ numbers, where n is the number of non-zero values and r is the number of rows. The above representation is CSR with absolute indices. Instead of storing the absolute position, we can compute the index difference and store the indices with relative

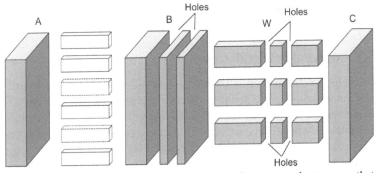

Fig. 6.2: Schematic diagram of pruning channel 1. B represents feature map that needs to be pruned. A represents the last feature map of B; W is the filter that needs to be pruned.

position. This representation requires $2n$ numbers. For further compression, one can restrict the number of bits (3 bits in this example) to represent the relative position and add a dummy zero weight when the relative position exceeds the largest value (8 for this example) that can be represented. These cases are called CSR with relative indices.

Unstructured pruning methods require additional software packages and hardware support due to the sparsity. While structured pruning belongs to coarse-grained pruning, and the model weight after pruning is not a sparse matrix, additional support is not required (Liu et al., 2018). The most typical structured pruning method is channel pruning (He et al., 2017). Figure 6.2 shows how channel pruning works. If two channels in the middle of feature map B are removed, the convolution channel corresponding to the convolution filter W is also removed. After removing the channels corresponding to the convolution kernels that generate feature map B, the amount of parameters will be significantly reduced, as shown in Fig. 6.2 for the holes. This channel-based pruning technology achieves the goal of model compression and accelerates the computing speed.

Yu et al. (2018) proposed a model pruning method by back-propagating an importance score to judge whether each neuron needs to be pruned. Other pruning algorithms have also been proposed. Molchanov et al. (2016) estimated the importance of each channel for pruning according to Taylor expansion Suau et al. (2020) proposed to prune redundant channels according to the internal connection between each layer. He et al. (2018) proposed a pruning method that can restore the pruned channel.

6.3 Knowledge Distillation

Knowledge distillation is to design a small student network and learn the knowledge from a teacher network without distinct performance loss. Compared with simple networks, complex networks usually have intuitive accuracy advantages. However, this advantage is not necessarily caused by the architecture gap between the two networks, but by the gap between the training difficulties (Buciluǎ et al., 2006). This is the premise that knowledge distillation can compress a large network into a small network. Knowledge distillation uses a lightweight network to imitate the teacher network, and obtains the knowledge of the model by approaching the soft output of the teacher network and improving the accuracy (Hinton et al., 2015). According to the location of the activated layer for learning, knowledge distillation can be divided into response-based knowledge distillation, feature-based knowledge distillation, and relation-based knowledge distillation. According to the stage of distillation, it can be divided into online distillation, offline distillation, and self-distillation.

6.3.1 Response-based Knowledge Distillation

Response-based knowledge distillation refers to training the student network based on the output of the last activation layer (Hinton et al., 2015). The structure of student network is simple and easy to deploy on edge devices. The generalization ability of teacher network is strong and can effectively extract the required features. Therefore, training the student network directly from features extracted by the teacher network can compress the model without obvious decrease in accuracy.

The output of traditional neural network after Softmax is closer to one hot coding, that is, the distribution of output is hard distribution. Since the output of the last activation layer does not pass through the Softmax layer, it is soft distribution and carries more valuable information which is more conducive to the training of student network. After obtaining the output of the activation layer, it is necessary to introduce a temperature T to control the extent of distribution softening. The improved Softmax function is $q_i = \dfrac{exp\,(z_i/T)}{\Sigma_j\,exp(z_i/T)}$. The loss function of training student network consists of two parts: the cross-entropy loss of the distribution difference between student network and teacher network, and the cross entropy loss between the output of student network and the real value. During training, the gradient is calculated according to the loss function, and then the gradient descent is used to update the parameters of the student network.

Softmax function with temperature T is used in training, and the traditional Softmax function is used in the inference stage to make the distribution closer to one hot coding. The disadvantage of this response-based knowledge distillation is that it pays too much attention to the output value of the last activation layer, neglecting the middle layers. Therefore, the method heavily relies on feature extraction of the teacher network (Gou et al., 2021).

6.3.2 Feature-based Knowledge Distillation

Unlike the response-based method, feature-based distillation focuses not only on the output of the last activation layer, but also on the output of the middle layers of the teacher network (Romero et al., 2021). By establishing the relationship between the middle layer of student network and teacher network, the student network would get closer to the teacher network, and function better. It should also be noted that selection of too many middle layers for the distillation will often lead to decrease of model accuracy. The loss function is:

$$\mathcal{L}_{HT}\,(W_G,\,W_r) = \frac{1}{2}\,\|u_h\,(x;\,W_H) - r(v_g\,(x;\,W_G);\_W_r)\|^2 \qquad (6.1)$$

where u_h refers to the activation value when the input of the teacher network is x and parameters are W_H. v_g refers to the activation value of the hidden layer when the input of the student network is x and the parameter is W_G. Since the size of the guided layer and the clue layer are not necessarily the same, it is necessary to temporarily add a fully connected layer or convolution layer after the guided layer to make their size consistent. r is the output of the added convolution layer or fully connected layer with parameter W_r as shown in Fig. 6.3.

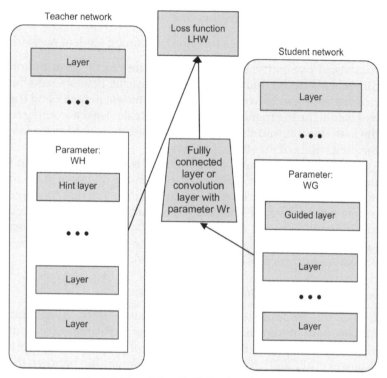

Fig. 6.3: Knowledge distillation based on feature.

Feature-based knowledge distillation needs to define the clue layer and guided layer, and update the parameters of student network by gradient descent. Then a response-based knowledge distillation is used on the output of the last activation layer to update the parameters of other network layers. Based on this, Zagoruyko et al. (2017) proposed attention-based distillation and added L2 normalized loss to the attention feature map between the clue layer and the guided layer, and calculated the gradient of the student network using back-propagation (Zagoruyko and Komodakis, 2017). Although feature-based knowledge distillation shows good performance in the training process, how to efficiently select clue layer and guided layer still needs further study (Jin et al., 2019).

6.3.3 Relation-based Knowledge Distillation

Relation-based knowledge distillation extracts the relationship between different activation layers in the teacher model, and the student model improves the accuracy by imitating this relationship between layers (Yim et al., 2017). The method of transforming hierarchical relation into feature matrix is to calculate the flow of solution procedure (FSP) matrix:

$$G_{ij}(x;W) = \sum_{s=1}^{h}\sum_{t=1}^{w} \frac{F_{s,t,i}^1(x;W) \times F_{s,t,j}^2(x;W)}{h \times w} \qquad (6.2)$$

$F_{s,t,i}^1(x;W)$ and $F_{s,t,j}^2(x;W)$ represent two activation layers of $w \times h \times m$ and $w \times h \times n$ matrices respectively. G is $n \times m$ FSP matrix, which is shown in Fig. 6.4.

It is assumed that the FSP matrix set generated by the teacher model is $G_i^t(i = 1,2, ..., p)$, FSP matrix set generated by the student

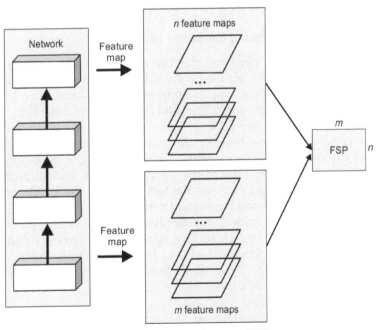

Fig. 6.4: Schematic diagram of FSP.

model is $G_i^s (i = 1, 2, ..., p)$, then the loss function based on the relationship is:

$$L_{FSP}(W_s, W_t) = \frac{1}{N} \sum_x \sum_{i=1}^n \lambda_i \times ||G_i^s(x; W_s) - G_i^t(x; W_t)||_2^2 \quad (6.3)$$

where λ_i is a self-defined weight. The training process is to train the teacher model and calculate the FSP matrix of the student model and the teacher model according to formula (6.3), optimize the student network according to formula (6.4), and finally fine-tune the parameters of the student network as a whole.

In addition to using FSP to represent the relationship between feature layers, Liu et al. (2017) used case relationship diagram to represent case features, the relationship between case features, and the transformation of feature space between layers. Chen et al. (2020) proposed a knowledge distillation method based on manifold learning. Passalis and Tefas et al. (2018) used probability distribution to represent the relationship between different layers.

6.3.4 *Other Algorithms of Knowledge Distillation*

Online distillation performs the training of teacher network and student network simultaneously. The advantage of online distillation is that it can train multiple student networks to build a student group at the same time, and the results are often better than offline distillation (Zhang et al., 2018). The loss functions are cross entropy loss between the real value and the predicted value plus the Kullback Leibler divergence (KL divergence) between Softmax outputs of the teacher network and student network. The training is to use the loss to update the weight of the teacher network and the student network. These two updates are carried out alternately. Self-distillation is a special type of online distillation of which student network is selected as a part of teacher network. One method is to divide the complex teacher network into several blocks. Each block is treated as a student network (Zhang et al., 2019).

6.4 Parameter Quantization

Parameter quantization aims to simplify the time and space complexity by converting floating-point data to integers. The main advantage of integer operation over floating-point operation is that it can improve the throughput of the system. The same register can process more values at one time, so as to speed up the forward operation. Parameter quantization can be Quantization Aware Training (QTA) (Tailor et al., 2020) and post training quantization (PTQ) (Liu et al., 2021) according to the stage of quantization. QTA parameter quantification occurs in the training and inference stages, while PTQ only occurs in the inference stage. The most common quantization is to convert float32 data into int8 data to participate in the forward operation. It is worth noting that at the model training stage, it does not perform quantization because a network with high accuracy can be obtained. Here, the forward operation of the fully connected layer is taken as an example to illustrate the process of parameter quantization (Jacob et al., 2018). The quantization of parameters satisfies $r = S(q - Z)$. r is the floating-point representation of data, and q is the integer data after data quantization. S is equivalent to the scale ratio between floating-point space and integer space. It is a floating-point data with the same type as r. Z is an offset in the integer space. For the multiplication of feature map and weight matrices, the whole forward process can be expressed as $q_3^{(i,k)} = Z_3 + M\sum_{j=i}^{N}(q_1^{(i,j)} - Z_1)(q_2^{(j,k)} - Z_2)$. $q_1^{(i,j)}$ and $q_2^{(i,j)}$ respectively represent required quantized feature values and quantized weights to calculate the output $q_3^{(i,k)}$ of the full connection layer in formula (7); only M is the floating-point data that needs to be represented by integer data. The formula for representing M is $M = 2^{-n} M_0$. The result of calculating the multiplication of two int8 number needs to be represented by int32 integer data, so we need a method to affine this data to int8 data. The whole quantization process is shown in Fig. 6.5.

In addition to the above methods, Polino proposed a model compression method combining knowledge distillation and parameter quantization, and the features of teacher network are transferred to student network to achieve a good result (Polino et al., 2018). Jacob et al. (2018) quantified both weight and the gradient estimated by Straight Through Estimator (STE) for back propagation. Based on such work, Fan et al. (2020) proposed a noise-based model compression method to further improve the compression accuracy. Different quantization methods are employed for different quantization data types.

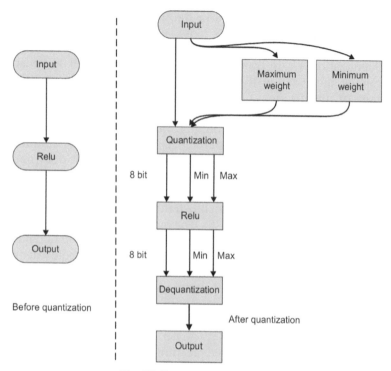

Fig. 6.5: Parameter quantization.

Chmiel et al. (2020) proposed a quantization method robust to different quantization data types.

6.5 Experiments

This section analyzes the model size, calculation efficiency, and performance of deep neural network, and then tests and analyzes the methods to improve the computational efficiency from model design and optimization. Firstly, the performances of different pruning methods are tested on object detection data sets MNIST, CIFAR and ImageNet. VGG-16 is used as the initial network for pruning, and the average values of precision, speed and parameters reduction of different methods are reported.

As shown in Table 6.1, each model pruning method has a significant parameter reduction, and the parameter amount of

Table 6.1: Performance comparison of parameter pruning methods.

Method	Parameters (unit: 10^6)	Accelerated ratio	Top-1 error increment (unit: %)	Top-5 error increment (unit: %)
VGG-16	138.4	1	0	0
L1-GAP (Li et al., 2016)	9.2	2.5	4.62	3.10
APoZ-GAP (Hu et al., 2016)	9.2	2.5	3.72	2.65
TE (Molchanov et al., 2016)	135.7	2.7	--	3.94
ThiNet (Luo et al., 2017)	9.5	2.3	1.00	0.52
ThiNet-T (Luo et al., 2017)	1.3	4.35	9.00	6.47

ThiNet was reduced by two orders of magnitude. The parameter reduction directly reduces the spatial complexity of the algorithm. However, the error increase rate of ThiNet is also large. From the perspective of computing acceleration, the speed increment is less than five times. In a word, model pruning can effectively reduce the memory consumption without significant performance loss, but the effect of computing acceleration is not that significant.

Table 6.2 shows the effect of different distillation methods on CIFAR10 data set. Each method reduces the parameter amount and efficiency without significant accuracy decrease. The reductions of parameter amount and processing time depend on the structure of teacher network and student network. In addition, because the compressed data is still floating-point data, the acceleration effect of forward operation is not distinct as that of parameter quantization.

Table 6.3 shows the effects of different parameter quantization methods on accuracy and acceleration. Parameter quantization converts floating-point data into integer data to speed up forward computing. BWN quantized the network weight into binary format, while XNOR-NET quantized weights and inputs at the same time. In Table 6.3, different parameter quantization methods show different results. XNOR-NET can accelerate the forward computing by 58 times, but it brings an error increase

Table 6.2: Performance comparison of knowledge distillation methods.

Method	Teacher network	Precision, # of parameters (unit: %, million)	Student network	Precision, # of parameters (unit: %, million)
FT (Kim et al., 2018)	ResNet56	93.61(0.85)	ResNet20	92.22(0.27)
Rocket-KD (Zhou et al., 2018)	WRN-40-1	93.42(0.6)	WRN-16-1	91.23(0.18)
DML (Zhang et al., 2019)	WRN-28-10	95.01(36.5)	ResNet32	92.47(0.46)
SP (Tung et al., 2019)	MobileNetV2	64.65(4.4)	MobileNetV2	63.38(2.2)

Table 6.3: Performance of parameter quantization.

Method	Top-1 error increase (unit %)	Top-5 error increase (unit %)	Accelerated ratio
BWN (Rastegari et al., 2016)	8.5	6.2	2
DoReFa-Net (Zhou et al., 2016)	10.1	7.7	--
XNOR-Net (Rastegari et al., 2016)	18.1	16.0	58

of 18.1%. Parameter quantization reduces the computational time but also brings accuracy loss. Therefore, it is necessary to select appropriate parameter quantification methods according to practical application situations.

6.6 Summary

Intelligent edge computing designs the lightweight neural network model through model compression. Knowledge distillation is an effective method to realize effective training of the lightweight model. Parameter quantization can further speed up the computational speed and the inference time. The model compression technologies discussed in this chapter are based on some classical networks in deep learning. Most of the related works study model compression from classical networks. With the development of deep learning, a more effective way is to directly design lightweight networks and deploy them on the edge.

In this book, we only discuss soft techniques for deep edge computing. In the future, the optimal intelligent computing system would combine both software and hardware advantages to maximize the computing power of intelligent hardware.

7
Conclusion and Discussion

In this book, we discuss deep learning algorithms design, model training, and model deployment techniques for crack-like object detection problem. Based on years of experience in pavement surface inspection system development, we introduce the related contents by addressing practical engineering problems in crack-like object detection. Specifically, we introduce detailed work and the process in addressing five important issues by using deep learning for industrial pavement crack detection and these have filled the gap between academic research and industrial application.

Specifically in Chapter 1, we introduce some basic knowledge related to this book, including deep learning, computer vision, object detection, crack detection, transfer learning, etc.

In Chapter 2, we employ a deep classification network for crack-region pre-selection which improved the performance by removing most of the noisy regions before crack segmentation. It conducts a pre-classification that detects and separates cracks and backgrounds in a region-based manner to separate the noisiest background from the regions of interest. Deep transfer learning is introduced to facilitate network training. Focusing on the target regions in a full image, threshold-based image segmentation is applied to find the cracks at pixel-level. Least Absolute Shrinkage and Selection Operator (LASSO) is employed to optimize the linear regression model to find the significant factors that affect the best segmentation threshold selection, and tensor voting is introduced to extract a complete crack curve for statistics.

In Chapter 3, we first generalized a classification network to a detection network with fully convolutional network, which realized one-stage crack detection for large-size input images. The method boosts the computation efficiency by more than 10 times faster than the window-sliding-based strategy, and makes deep learning feasible for real-time industrial crack detection. The work discussed in this chapter is the first work which performs pixel-level crack detection in an end-to-end mode with industrial pavement crack image. A classification network classifies an image block as crack or background. Weak supervised learning and fully convolutional network are used to convert a classification network into an object detection network that is insensitive to the input size. The equivalent dense-dilation design enables the transfer of both low-level and middle-level knowledge from the classification network to facilitate the end-to-end network refining and improve the crack localization accuracy.

In Chapter 4, we introduce generative adversarial learning to solve an important problem inherent in crack-like object detection, data imbalance. This chapter proposes Crack-Patch-Only (CPO) supervised generative adversarial learning for end-to-end training, which forces the network to always produce crack-GT images while reserving both crack and BG-image translation abilities by feeding a larger-size crack image into an asymmetric U-shape generator to overcome the 'All Black' issue. The network is robust to biased GTs, which greatly reduces the workload of preparing GTs for training. It is of great significance in reducing labor-costs and the budget in industry applications. The chapter provides a concrete example by utilizing generative adversarial learning to resolve practical problems and is also the first work to perform object regularization by providing a loss that is from data training instead of hand-made regularization term.

In Chapter 5, we propose a self-supervised method for crack detection. It discusses a self-supervised structure learning network which can be trained without using paired data. A labor-free structure library is prepared and set as the target domain for structure learning, and a dual-network is built with two GANs: one is trained to translate a crack image patch (X) to a structural patch (Y), and the other is trained to translate (Y) back to (X), simultaneously. The work formulates crack detection as a structure learning problem which provides a new thread for automatic deep crack detection. The method introduces cycle-consistent generative adversarial networks that do not need to manually prepare GTs for training, which is an important research direction of the future system for crack detection.

In Chapter 6, we discuss soft techniques of deep edge computing, including parameter pruning, knowledge distillation, and parameter quantization for constructing lightweight networks. The techniques are the main means to implement an efficient deep learning model on the edge with limited computational resources, such as mobile phones. Parameter pruning is used to reduce the parameter amount which results in memory cost reduction and also speeding up of computing. Knowledge distillation is an important method to succeed in the training of lightweight network. Parameter quantization simplifies time and space complexity by converting floating-point data to integers.

The book focuses on deep learning for crack-like object detection problems based on the pavement crack detection; nonetheless, the proposed method can be used for multi-class object detection via setting the output of layer as multi-channels, such as locating road marks, discriminating crack and sealed cracks, etc.

We propose to use generative adversarial learning for crack detection. However, it should be mentioned that the networks detect the cracks as n-width crack curves which will miss the crack width information. In practical applications, many of the protocols prefer to use crack width to estimate cracking severity, which might be an issue for the proposed methods, and this needs to be further discussed.

References

Abdel, I., O. Abudayyeh, and M.E. Kelly. (2003). Analysis of edge-detection techniques for crack identification in bridges. *J. Comput. Civil Eng.*, 17(4): 255–263.

Alekseychuk, O. (2005). Detection of crack-like indications in digital radiography by global optimization of a probabilistic estimation function. Ph.D. thesis, Dresden Univ. of Technology, Dresden, Germany.

Amhaz, R., S. Chambon, J. Idier, and V. Baltazart. (2016). Automatic crack detection on two-dimensional pavement images: An algorithm based on minimal path selection. *IEEE Trans. Intell. Transp. Syst.*, 17(10): 2718–2729.

Anwar, S., K. Hwang, and Sung, W. (2017). Structured pruning of deep convolutional neural networks. *ACM Journal on Emerging Technologies in Computing Systems (JETC)*, 13(3): 1–18.

Buciluǎ, C., R. Caruana, and A. Niculescu-Mizil. (2006). Model compression. *Proceedings of the 12th ACM SIGKDD*, 2006: 535–541.

Central Intelligence Agency (CIA) (2017, Jan.). *The World Fact Book*, https://www.cia.gov/library/publications/resources/the-world-factbook/.

Cha, Y.J., W. Choi, and O. Büyüköztürk. (2017). Deep learning-based crack damage detection using convolutional neural networks. *Computer-aided Civil and Infrastructure Engineering*, 32(5): 361–378.

Chan, K.B., S. Soetandio and R.L. Lytton. (1989). Distress identification by an automatic thresholding technique. *Proc., Int. Conf. on Application of Advanced Technologies in Transportation Engineering*, San Diego.

Chen, D., J.P. Mei, Y. Zhang et al. (2021). Cross-layer distillation with semantic calibration. *The Proceedings of the AAAI*, 2021: 7028–7036.

Chen, H., Y. Wang, C. Xu et al. (2019). Data-free learning of student networks. *The Proceedings of IEEE CVPR*, 2019: 3514–3522.

Chen, H., Y. Wang, C. Xu et al. (2020). Learning student networks via feature embedding. *IEEE Transactions on Neural Networks and Learning Systems*, 32(1): 25–35.

Chen, L.C., G. Papandreou, I. Kokkinos et al. (2015). Semantic image segmentation with deep convolutional nets and fully connected CRFs. *The Proceedings of ICLR*.

Chen, L., G. Papandreou, I. Kokkinos et al. (2017). DeepLab: Semantic image segmentation with deep convolutional nets, atrous convolution, and fully connected CRFs. *arXiv preprint arXiv:1606.00915*.

Cheng, H.D., and M. Miyojim. (1998). Novel system for automatic pavement distress detection. *J. Comput. Civil Eng.*, **12**(3): 145–152.

Cheng, H.D., J. Chen, C. Glazier, and Y.G. Hu. (1999a). Novel approach to pavement crack detection based on fuzzy set theory. *J. Comput. Civil Eng.*, **13**(4): 270–280.

Cheng, H.D., J. Wang, Y. Hu et al. (1999b). Novel approach to pavement cracking detection based on neural network. *Transp. Res. Rec.*, **1764**: 119–127.

Cheng, H.D., J. Wang, Y. Hu, C. Glazier, X. Shi and X. Chen. (2001). Novel approach to pavement cracking detection based on neural network. *Transp. Res. Rec.*, **1764**: 119–127.

Chmiel, B., R. Banner, and G. Shomron et al. (2020). Robust quantization: one model to rule them all. *The Proceedings of Advances in Neural Information Processing Systems*, **33**: 5308–5317.

Cho, J.H., and B. Hariharan. (2019). On the efficacy of knowledge distillation. *The Proceedings of the IEEE/CVF International Conference on Computer Vision*.

Dai, J., Y. Li, and K. He et al. (2016). R-FCN: Object detection via region-based fully convolutional networks. *arXiv preprint arXiv:1605.06409*.

Dalal, N., and B. Triggs. (2005). Histograms of oriented gradients for human detection. *The Proceedings of IEEE CVPR*.

Deng, J., W. Dong, R. Socher et al. (2009). Imagenet: A large-scale hierarchical image database. *The Proceedings of IEEE Conference on Computer Vision and Pattern Recognition*.

Doersch, C., A. Gupta, and A.A. Efros. (2015). Unsupervised visual representation learning by context prediction. *The Proceedings of IEEE ICCV*.

Doersch, C., and A. Zisserman. (2017). Multi-task self-supervised visual learning. *arXiv preprint arXiv:1708.07860*.

Dollár, P., and C.L. Zitnick. (2013). Structured forests for fast edge detection. *The Proceedings of IEEE ICCV*.

Everingham, M., L.V. Gool, C.K.I. William et al. (2011). The PASCAL Visual Object Classes Challenge 2011 Results. *http://www.pascalnetwork.org/challenges/VOC/voc2011/workshop/index.html*.

F.H.A. (2006). Pavement distress identification manual, *NPS Road Inventory Program*.

Fan, A., P. Stock, B. Graham et al. (2020). Training with quantization noise for extreme model compression. *arXiv preprint arXiv:2004.07320*.

Friedman, J., T. Hastie, and R. Tibshirani. (2010). Regularization paths for generalized linear models via coordinate descent. *J. Stat. Software*, **33**(1): 1–22.

Fukui, H., T. Hirakawa, T. Yamashita et al. (2019). Attention branch network: Learning of attention mechanism for visual explanation. *The Proceedings of the IEEE Conference on Computer Vision and Pattern Recognition*.

Ganin, Y., and V. Lempitsky. (2014). Unsupervised domain adaptation by backpropagation. *arXiv preprint arXiv:1409.7495*.

Gavilan, M., D. Balcones, D.F. Llorca et al. (2011). Adaptive road crack detection system by pavement classification. *Sensors*, **11**(10): 9628–9657.

Girshick, R. (2015). Fast R-CNN. *The proceedings of IEEE ICCV*.

Girshick, R., J. Donahue, T. Darrell et al. (2014). Rich feature hierarchies for accurate object detection and semantic segmentation. *The Proceedings of IEEE CVPR*.

Gonzalez, R.C., R.E. Woods, and S.L. Steven. (2009). *Digital Image Processing Using Matlab*, Addison-Wesley.

Goodfellow, I.J., J. Pouget-Abadie, M. Mirza et al. (2014). Generative adversarial nets. *The Proceedings of NIPS*.

Gou, J., B. Yu, S.J. Maybank et al. (2021). Knowledge distillation: A survey. *International Journal of Computer Vision*, **129**(6): 1789–1819.

Gupta, S., J. Hoffman, and J. Malik. (2016). Cross modal distillation for supervision transfer, *The Proceedings of the IEEE Conference on Computer Vision and Pattern Recognition*, 2016: 2827–2836.

Han, K., A. Xiao, E. Wu, et al. (2021). Transformer in transformer. *The Proceedings of Advances in Neural Information Processing Systems*.

Han, S., J. Pool, J. Tran et al. (2015). Learning both weights and connections for efficient neural network. *The Proceedings of Neural Information Processing Systems*, 2015: 1135–1143.

Hariharan, B., P. Arbelaez, R. Grishick et al. (2014). Simultaneous detection and segmentation. *The Proceedings of ECCV*.

Hassibi, B., D.G. Stork, and G.J. Wolff. (1993). Optimal brain surgeon and general network pruning. *IEEE International Conference on Neural Networks*, 1993: 293–299.

Hawks, N.F., and T.P. Teng. (2014). *Distress Identification Manual for the Long-term Pavement Performance Project*. National Academy of Sciences.

He, K., X. Zhang, S. Ren, and J. Sun. (2014). Spatial pyramid pooling in deep convolutional networks for visual recognition. *The Proceedings of ECCV*, Springer.

He, K., G. Gkioxari, P. Dollar, et al. (2017). Mask R-CNN. *arXiv preprint arXiv:1703.06870*.

He, Y., X. Zhang, and J. Sun. (2017). Channel pruning for accelerating very deep neural networks. *The Proceedings of IEEE International Conference on Computer Vision*, 2017: 1389–1397.

He, Y., G. Kang, X. Dong et al. (2018). Soft filter pruning for accelerating deep convolutional neural networks. *The Proceedings of IJCAI*, 2018: 2234–2240.

Hinton, G.E., and R.R. Salakhutdinov. (2006). Reducing the dimensionality of data with neural networks, *Science*, **313**(5786): 504–507.

Hinton, G.E., S. Osindero, and Y.W. The (2006). A fast learning algorithm for deep belief nets, *Neural Comput.*, **18**(7): 1527–1554.

Hinton, G.E., D. Li, Y. Dong et al. (2012). Deep neural networks for acoustic modeling in speech recognition: The shared views of four groups. *IEEE Signal Process. Mag.*, **29**(6): 82–97.

Hinton, G., Vinyals, O., and Dean, J. (2015). Distilling the knowledge in a neural network. *The Proceedings of International Conference on NIPS*.

Hirschberg, J., and C.D. Manning. (2015). Advances in natural language processing. *Science*, **349**(6245): 261–266.

Howard, A.G., M. Zhu, B. Chen et al. (2017). Mobilenets: Efficient convolutional neural networks for mobile vision applications. *arXiv preprint arXiv:1704.04861*.

Hu, H., R. Peng, Y.W. Tai et al. (2016). Network trimming: A data-driven neuron pruning approach towards efficient deep architectures. *arXiv preprint arXiv:1607.03250*.

Hu, Y., and C.X. Zhao. (2010). A local binary pattern-based methods for pavement crack detection. *J. Pattern Recognit. Res.*, **5**(1): 140–147.

Huang, Y., and B. Xu. (2006). Automatic inspection of pavement cracking distress. *Journal of Electronic Imaging*, **15**(1): 17–27.

Isola, P., J.Y. Zhu, T. Zhou et al. (2017). Image-to-image translation with conditional adversarial networks. *The Proceedings of IEEE CVPR*.

Jacob, B., S. Kligys, B. Chen et al. (2018). Quantization and training of neural networks for efficient integer-arithmetic-only inference. *The Proceedings of the IEEE Conference on Computer Vision and Pattern Recognition*, 2018: 2704–2713.

Jarvis, R.A. (1983). A perspective on range finding techniques for computer vision. *IEEE Transactions on Pattern Analysis and Machine Intelligence*, **5**(2): 122–139.

Jia, Y., E. Shelhamer, J. Donahue, S. Karayev et al. (2014). Caffe: Convolutional architecture for fast feature embedding. *ArXiv preprint arXiv: 1408. 5093*.

Jin, X, B. Peng, Y. Wu et al. (2019). Knowledge distillation via route constrained optimization. *The Proceedings of the IEEE CVPR*, 2019: 1345–1354.

Joachims, T. (1998). Text categorization with support vector machines: Learning with many relevant features. *The Proceedings of European Conference on Machine Learning*.

Kaelbling, L.P., M.L. Littman, and A.W. Moore. (1996). Reinforcement learning: A survey. *Journal of Artificial Intelligence Research*, **4**: 237–285.

Kaul, V., A. Yezzi, and Y.C. Tai. (2010). Quantitative performance evaluation algorithms for pavement distress segmentation. *Transp. Res. Rec.*, **2153**: 106–113.

Kim, J., S.U. Park and N. Kwak. (2018). Paraphrasing complex network: Network compression via factor transfer. *The Proceedings of NIPS*.

Kingma, D.P., and J. Ba. (2014). Adam: A method for stochastic optimization. *arXiv preprint arXiv:1412.6980*.

Kirschke, K.R., and S.A. Velinsky. (1992). Histogram-based approach for automated pavement crack sensing. *Journal of Transportation Engineering*, **118**(5): 700–710.

Kontschieder, P., S.R. Bulo, and M. Pelillo. (2011). Structured class-labels in random forest for semantic image labeling. *The Proceedings of IEEE ICCV*, 2190–2197.

Koutsopoulos, H.N., I.E. Sanhouri, and A.B. Downey. (1993). Analysis of segmentation algorithms for pavement distress images. *Journal of Transportation Engineering*, **119**(6): 868–888.

Krizhevsky, A., I. Sutskever, and G.E. Hinton. (2012). ImageNet classification with deep convolutional neural network. *The Proceedings of NIPS*.

Lad, P., and M. Pawar. (2016). Evaluation of railway track crack detection system. *The Proceedings of the IEEE ROMA*.

Laurent, C., C. Ballas, T. George et al. (2020). Revisiting loss modelling for unstructured pruning. *arXiv preprint arXiv:2006.12279*.

Lecun, Y., B. Boser, J.S. Denker, D. Henderson, R.E. Howard, W. Hubbard and L.D. Jackel. (1989). Backpropagation applied to handwritten zip code recognition. *Neural Computation*, 1(4): 541–551.

LeCun, Y., Y. Bengio, and G. Hinton (2015). Deep learning. *Nature*, 521: 436–444.

Li, H., D. Song, Y. Liu, and B. Li. (2018). Automatic pavement crack detection by multi-scale image fusion, *IEEE Trans. Intell. Transp. Syst. Doi: 10.1109/TITS.2018.2856928*.

Li, H., A. Kadav, I. Durdanovic et al. (2016). Pruning filters for efficient convnets. *arXiv preprint arXiv:1608.08710*.

Linton, T. (2017). *Tensor Voting.* https://www.mathworkcia.gov/library/publications/resources.

Liu, W., D. Anguelov, D. Erhan, C. Szegedy et al. (2016). SSD: Single shot multi-box detector. *The Proceedings* of *ECCV*, Springer.

Liu, Y., J. Cao, B. Li et al. (2019). Knowledge distillation via instance relationship graph. *The Proceedings of the IEEE CVPR*, 2019: 7096–7104.

Liu, Y., M.M. Cheng, X. Hu et al. (2017). Richer convolutional features for edge detection, *The Proceedings of IEEE CVPR*.

Liu, Z., M. Sun, T. Zhou et al. (2018). Rethinking the value of network pruning. *arXiv preprint arXiv:1810.05270*.

Liu, Z., Y. Wang, K. Han et al. (2021). Post-training quantization for vision transformer. *The Proceedings of International Conference on Neural Information Processing Systems*.

Long, J., E. Shelhamer, and T. Darrell. (2015). Fully convolutional networks for semantic segmentation. *The Proceedings of IEEE CVPR*.

Luo, J.H., Wu, J., and Lin, W. (2017). Thinet: A filter level pruning method for deep neural network compression. *The Proceedings of the IEEE International Conference on Computer Vision*, 2017: 5058–5066.

Ma, X., S. Lin, S. Ye et al. (2021). Non-structured DNN weight pruning – Is it beneficial in any platform? *IEEE Transactions on Neural Networks and Learning Systems*.

Maeda, H., Y. Sekimoto, T. Seto et al. (2018). Road damage detection and classification using deep neural networks with smartphone images, *Computer-aided Civil and Infrastructure Engineering*, 33(12): 1127–1141.

Martin, D., C. Fowlkes, D. Tal et al. (2001). A database of human segmented natural images and its application to evaluating segmentation algorithms and measuring ecological statistics. *The Proceedings of IEEE ICCV*.

Medioni, G., and C. Tang. (2000). Tensor Voting: Theory and Applications,. *The Proceedings of 12th Congress Francophone AFRIF-AFIA de Reconnaissance des Formes et Intelligence Artificial*.

Mirza, M., and S. Osindero. (2014). Conditional generative adversarial nets. *arXiv preprint arXiv:1411.1784*.

Molchanov, P., S. Tyree, T. Karras et al. (2016). Pruning convolutional neural networks for resource efficient inference. *arXiv preprint arXiv:1611.06440*.

Nair, V., and Hinton, G.E. (2010). Rectified linear units improve restricted Boltzmann machines. *The Proceedings of ICML*.

Nejad, F.M., and H. Zakeri. (2011). A comparison of multi-resolution methods for detection and isolation of pavement distress. *Journal of Expert Systems with Applications*, 38(3): 2857–2872.

Nguyen, T.S., S. Begot, F. Duculty et al. (2011). Free-form anisotropy: A new method for crack detection on pavement surface images. *The Proceedings of IEEE ICIP*.

Nocedal, J., and S.J. Wright. (2020). *Numerical Optimization*, Springer.

Noroozi, M. and P. Favaro. (2016). Unsupervised learning of visual representations by solving jigsaw puzzles. *In Proc., ECCV*. Berlin, Germany: Springer.

Noroozi, M., and P. Favaro. (2016). Unsupervised learning of visual representations by solving jigsaw puzzles. *The Proceedings of ECCV*.

Oliveira, H., and P.L. Correia. (2009). Automatic road crack segmentation using entropy and dynamic thresholding. *The Proceedings of 17th European Signal Processing Conf.*, 2009: 622–626.

Oliveira, H., and P.L. Correia. (2014). CrackIT—An image processing toolbox for crack detection and characterization. *The Proceedings of IEEE ICIP.*

Oquab, M., L. Bottou, I. Laptev et al. (2014). Learning and transferring mid-level image representations. *The Proceedings of IEEE CVPR.*

Otsu, N. (1975). A threshold selection method from gray-level histograms. *IEEE Trans. Syst. Man Cybern.*, 9(1): 62–66.

Otsu, N. (1979). A threshold selection method from gray-level histograms., *IEEE Trans. on Syst. Man Cybern.*, **9**(1): 62–66.

Pan, S.J., and Q. Yang. (2010). A survey on transfer learning. *IEEE Trans. on Knowl. Data Eng.*, **22**(10): 1345–1359.

Passalis, N., and A. Tefas. (2018). Learning deep representations with probabilistic knowledge transfer. *The Proceedings of the European Conference on Computer Vision*, 2018: 268–284.

Petrou, M., and J. Kittler. (1996). Automatic surface crack detection on textured materials. *J. Mater. Process. Technol.*, **56**(4): 158–167.

Polino, A., Pascanu, R., and Alistarh, D. (2018). Model compression via distillation and quantization. *arXiv preprint arXiv:1802.05668.*

Power, D. (2011). Evaluation: from precision, recall and F-measure to ROC, Informedness, markedness and correlation. *Journal of Machine Learning Technologies*, **2**(1): 37–63.

Radford, A., L. Metz, and S. Chintala. (2016). Unsupervised representation learning with deep convolutional generative adversarial networks. *The Proceedings of ICLR.*

Rastegari, M., Ordonez, V., Redmon, J. et al. (2016). Xnor-net: Imagenet classification using binary convolutional neural networks. *The Proceedings of ECCV*, Springer, Cham, 2016: 525–542.

Redmon, J., S. Divvala, R. Girshick et al. (2015). You only look once: Unified, real-time object detection. *arXiv preprint arXiv:1506.02640.*

Redmon, J., and A. Farhadi. (2017). YOLO9000: Better, faster, stronger. *The Proceedings of IEEE CVPR.*

Ren, S., K. He, R. Girshick et al. (2015). Faster R-CNN: Towards real-time object detection with region proposal networks. *arXiv preprint arXiv:1506.01497.*

Romero, A., N. Ballas, S.E. Kahou et al. (2015). Fitnets: Hints for thin deep nets. *The Proceedings of ICLR.*

Ronneberger, O., P. Fischer, and T. Brox. (2015). U-Net: Convolutional networks for biomedical image segmentation. *The Proceedings of in Proc. Med. Image Comput. Comput.-assist. Intervention.*

Rosenfield, A., and R.C. Smith. (1979). Thresholding using relaxation. *IEEE Transactions on Pattern Analysis and Machine Intelligence*, 3(5): 598–606.

Rumelhart, D.E., G.E. Hinton, and R.J. Williams. (1986). Learning representations by back-propagating errors, *Nature*, **323**(6088): 533–536.

Schraudolph, N.N. (2002). Fast curvature matrix-vector products for second-order gradient descent. *Neural Computation*, 14(7): 1723–1738.

Sermanet, P., D. Eigen, X. Zhang et al. (2014). Overfeat: Integrated recognition, localization and detection using convolutional networks. *arXive prepring arXiv:1312.6229.*

Sheather, S.J. (2009). *A modern approach to regression with R*, Springer, New York.

Shi, Y., L. Cui, F. Meng and Z.S. Chen. (2016). Automatic road crack detection using random structured forest. *IEEE Trans. on Intelligent Transportation Systems*, **17**(12): 3434–3445.

Simonyan, K., and A. Zisserman. (2014). Very deep convolutional networks for large-scale image recognition. *CoRR, abs/1409.1556.*

Sohn, K., S. Liu, G. Zhong et al. (2017). Unsupervised domain adaptation for face recognition in unlabeled videos. *The Proceedings of IEEE CVPR.*

Song, H., W. Wang, F. Wang et al. (2015). Pavement crack detection by ridge detection on fractional calculus and dual-thresholds. *International Journal of Multimedia and Ubiquitous Engineering*, **10**(4): 19–30.

Srivastava, N., G. Hinton, A. Krizhevsky et al. (2014). Dropout: A simple way to prevent neural networks from overfitting. *The Journal of Machine Learning Research*, **15**(1): 1929–1958.

Suau, X., L. Zappella, V. Palakkode et al. (2020). Principal filter analysis for guided network compression. *The Proceedings of WACV*, 2020: 3140–3149.

Tailor, S.A., J. Fernandez-Marques, and N.D. Lane. (2020). Degree-quant: Quantization-aware training for graph neural networks. *arXiv preprint arXiv:2008.05000.*

Tibshirani, R. (1996). Regression shrinkage and selection via lasso. *Journal of Royal Statistic Society*, **58**(1): 267–288.

Tran, L., X. Yin, and X. Liu. (2017). Disentangled representation learning GAN for pose-invariant face recognition. *The Proceedings of IEEE CVPR.*

Tsai, Y.C., V. Kaul, and R.M. Mersereau. (2010). Critical assessment of pavement distress segmentation methods. *Journal of Transportation Engineering*, **136**(1): 11–19.

Tsai, Y.C., and A. Chatterjee. (2017). Comprehensive, quantitative crack detection algorithm performance evaluation system. *J. Comput. Civ. Eng.*, **31**(5): 04017047.

Tung, F., and, G. Mori. (2019). Similarity-preserving knowledge distillation. *The Proceedings of the IEEE ICCV*, 2019: 1365–1374.

Uijlings, J., K. Van de Sande, T. Gevers, and A. Smeulders. (2013). Selective search for object recognition. *Int. J. Comput. Vision*, **104**(2): 154–171.

Vaheesan, K., C. Chandrakumar, and M. Rahman. (2015). Tiled fuzzy Hough transform for crack detection. *The Proceedings of 12th International Conference on Quality Control by Artificial Vision*, SPIE(953411): 1–6.

Wan, L., M. Zeiler, S. Zhang et al. (2013). Regularization of neural networks using DropConnect. *The Proceedings of ICML.*

Wang, C.Y., H.Y.M. Liao, Y.H. Wu et al. (2020). CSPNet: A new backbone that can enhance learning capability of CNN. *Proceedings of IEEE Conference on Computer Vision and Pattern Recognition Workshops.*

Wang, C., R. Grosse, S. Fidler et al. (2019). Eigendamage: Structured pruning in the Kronecker-factored Eigenbasis. *The Proceedings of International Conference on Machine Learning*, 2019: 6566–6575.

Wang, K., Li Q., and W. Gong. (2000). Wavelet-based pavement distress image edge detection with a trous algorithm. *Transp. Res. Rec.*, **6**(2024): 24–32.

Wang, W. (2015). Protocol based pavement cracking measurement with 1 mm 3D pavement surface model, Ph.D. thesis, Oklahoma State Univ., Stillwater.

Wu, Z., C. Shen, and A. Van Den Hengel. (2019). Wider or deeper: Revisiting the resnet model for visual recognition. *Pattern Recognition*, 90: 119–133.

Xie, S., and Z. Tu. (2015). Holistically-nested edge detection. *The Proceedings of ICCV*.

Yang, X., H. Li, Y. Yu et al. (2018). Automatic pixel-level crack detection and measurement using fully convolutional network. *Comput.-Aided Civ. Infrastructure. Eng.*, **33**(12): 1090–1109.

Yim, J., D. Joo, J. Bae et al. (2017). A gift from knowledge distillation: Fast optimization, network minimization and transfer learning. *The Proceedings of the IEEE Conference on Computer Vision and Pattern Recognition*, 2017: 4133–4141.

Yosinski, J., J. Clune, Y. Bengio et al. (2014). How transferable are features in deep neural networks? *The Proceedings of NIPS*.

Yu, F., and V. Koltun. (2016). Multi-scale context aggregation by dilated convolutions. *The Proceedings of ICLR*.

Yu, R., A. Li, C.F. Chen et al. (2018). NIPS: Pruning networks using neuron importance score propagation. *The Proceedings of the IEEE Conference on Computer Vision and Pattern Recognition*, 2018: 9194–9203.

Zagoruyko, S., and N. Komodakis. (2017). Paying more attention to attention: Improving the performance of convolutional neural networks via attention transfer. *The Proceedings of ICLR*.

Zalama, E., J. Bermejo, R. Medina, and J. Llamas (2014). Road crack detection using visual features extracted by Gabor filters., *Computer-aided Civil and Infrastructure Engineering*, **29**(5): 342–358.

Zeng, W., and Urtasun, R. (2018). MLPrune: Multi-layer pruning for automated neural network compression. *The Proceedings of International Conference on Learning Representation*.

Zhang, A., C.P. Kelvin, B. Wang et al. (2017). Automated pixel-level pavement crack detection on 3D asphalt surfaces using a deep-learning network, *Comput.-aided Civ. Infrastruct. Eng.*, **32**(10): 805–819.

Zhang, K.G., and H.D. Cheng. (2017). A novel pavement crack detection approach using pre-selection based on transfer learning. *The Proceedings of the 9th International Conference on Image and Graphics*, Shanghai, China.

Zhang, K.G., H.D. Cheng, and B. Zhang. (2018). Unified approach to pavement crack and sealed crack detection using pre-classification based on transfer learning. *J. Comput. Civil Eng.*, **32**(2): 04018001.

Zhang, K.G., H.D. Cheng, and S. Gai. (2018). Efficient dense-dilation network for pavement crack detection with large input image size. *The Proceedings of the IEEE ITSC*, Hawaii, USA.

Zhang, K.G., Y.T. Zhang, and H.D. Cheng. (2020). Self-supervised structure learning for crack detection based on cycle-consistent generative adversarial networks. *J. Comput. Civil Eng.*, 34(3): 04020004.

Zhang, K.G., Y.T. Zhang, and H.D. Cheng. (2021). CrackGAN: Pavement crack detection using partially accurate ground truths based on generative adversarial learning. *IEEE Transactions on Intelligent Transportation Systems*, 22(2): 1306–1319.

Zhang, L., F. Yang, Y.D. Zhang, and Y.J. Zhu. (2016). Road crack detection using deep convolutional neural network. *The Proceedings of IEEE ICIP*, Beijing, China.

Zhang, L., J. Song, A. Gao et al. (2019). Be your own teacher: Improve the performance of convolutional neural networks via self-distillation. *The Proceedings of IEEE CVPR*, 2019: 3713–3722.

Zhang, X., X. Zhou, M. Lin et al. (2018). ShuffleNet: An extremely efficient convolutional neural network for mobile devices. *The Proceedings of the IEEE Conference on Computer Vision and Pattern Recognition*.

Zhang, Y., T. Xiang, T.M. Hospedales et al. (2018). Deep mutual learning. *The Proceedings of the IEEE Conference on Computer Vision and Pattern Recognition*, 2018: 4320–4328.

Zhou, G., Y. Fan, R. Cui et al. (2018). Rocket launching: A universal and efficient framework for training well-performing light net. *The Proceedings of the AAAI*.

Zhou, J., P.S. Huang, and F.P. Chiang. (2006). Wavelet-based pavement distress detection evaluation. *Optic Engineering*, **45**(2): 1–10.

Zhou, S., Wu, Y., Ni, Z. et al. (2016). Dorefa-net: Training low bitwidth convolutional neural networks with low bitwidth gradients. *arXiv preprint arXiv:1606.06160*.

Zhu, J., T. Park, P. Isola, and A.A. Efros. (2017). Unpaired image-to-image translation using cycle-consistent adversarial networks. *The Proceedings of IEEE ICCV*.

Zou, Q., Z. Zhang, Q. Li et al. (2019). DeepCrack: learning hierarchical convolutional features for crack detection. *IEEE Trans. on Image Processing*.

Zou, Q., Y. Cao, Q. Li, Q. Mao, and S. Wang. (2012). CrackTree: Automatic crack detection from pavement images, *Pattern Recognition Letters*, **33**(3): 227–238.

Index

.